1,999

FACTS ABOUT BLACKS

A Sourcebo
African-American A

Second Editi

D1517956

Raymond M. Corbin

Madison Books
Lanham • New York • London

Published by Madison Books
4720 Boston Way
Lanham, Maryland 20706

3 Henrietta Street
London WC2E 8LU, England

Library of Congress Cataloging-in-Publication Data

Corbin, Raymond M.
     1,999 Facts about Blacks : a sourcebook of African-American
achievement / Raymond M. Corbin. — 2nd ed.
          p.   cm.
     Includes index.
     ISBN 1-56833-081-2 (pbk. : alk. paper)
     1. Afro-Americans—Miscellanea.   I. Title.
E185.C83   1997
973'.0496073—dc20   96-34904
                                                           CIP

ISBN 1-56833-081-2 (pbk. : alk. paper)

Distributed by National Book Network

⊖™ The paper used in this publication meets the minimum requirements of
American National Standard for Information Sciences—Permanence of
Paper for Printed Library Materials, ANSI Z39.48–1984.
Manufactured in the United States of America.

To my mother, Mrs. Pearl Corbin; to a very dear friend, Mary Sutton for her patience; Loretta Sutton for typing, and a special friend, Richard White who stood by me all the way. I would also like to thank Barry Beckham who was not only the publisher of the first edition but also has been a good friend for over thirty years. To all of you: thank you very much.

Contents

Abbreviations

ACT-SO	Afro-Academic, Cultural, Technological, Scientific Olympics
CORE	Congress of Racial Equality
HUD	Housing and Urban Development
NAACP	National Association for the Advancement of Colored People
NOW	National Organization of Women
Ph.D.	Doctor of Philosophy
PUSH	People United to Save Humanity
SCLC	Southern Christian Leadership Conference
SNCC	Student Non-Violent Coordinating Committee

Introduction

Here is the second edition of *1,999 Facts about Blacks*. Approximately one third of these facts are achievements since 1986 when the first edition was published.

The new design places the answers at the bottom of the page rather than at the back of the book. I've also included a bibliography for those who want to pursue African-American history beyond the question-and-answer phase.

Please write to me at Madison Books if you have corrections, additions, or suggestions, or if you want information about my upcoming newsletter on black history.

Enjoy—and learn.

Raymond M. Corbin
July 1996

History

1. Who was the first African-American press secretary for a First Lady in 1989?

2. By November 1992 the National Brotherhood of Skiers had 14,000 members in how many states?

3. What was the first item ever patented by an African-American inventor?

4. In 1974 she became the first black woman named a White House Fellow.

5. In what state was the National Bar Association orgainized by twelve African-American lawyers?

6. He is considered the first to die in the Boston Massacre of 1770.

7. He was Chicago's first wholesaler, first merchant prince, and its first settler.

8. Who, in 1834, was the first African-American to receive a U.S. patent?

1. Anna Perez

2. 22

3. Corn planter

4. Barbara W. Hancock

5. Iowa

6. Crispus Attucks

7. Jean Baptiste Point DuSable

8. Henry Blair

9. Which state became the first to abolish slavery in 1777?

10. Who founded the North Carolina Mutual Life Insurance Company?

11. Between 1872 and 1920 he received over 57 patents for automatic lubricating appliances.

12. What was the name of the newspaper published by Frederick Douglass?

13. He performed a successful Siamese twin operation at Johns Hopkins Hospital in 1987.

14. What does CORE stand for?

15. In what year did the Birmingham Civil Rights Institute open?

16. He was the first black awarded the Nobel Peace prize.

17. She would not move to the back of the bus in Montgomery, Alabama, in 1955.

18. Who was the first president of the Southern Christian Leadership Conference?

19. Who was called "the Black Edison?"

20. In 1988 this reporter and author was the first black to deliver a commencement address at the University of Georgia.

9. Vermont

10. John Merrick

11. Elijah McCoy

12. *The North Star*

13. Benjamin Carson

14. The Congress of Racial Equality

15. 1992

16. Ralph J. Bunche

17. Rosa Parks

18. Martin Luther King Jr.

19. Granville T. Woods

20. Charlayne Hunter-Gault

21. Which city was the first to pass laws against racial or religious discrimination in housing in 1957?

22. In 1992 she became the first African-American woman to be appointed Secretary of Energy.

23. This leader of the Nation of Islam called for the creation of a black state in the United States in 1960.

24. In 1992 she became the highest-ranking woman in the U.S. Marine Corps.

25. Who founded the Organization for Afro-American Unity in 1964?

26. What is the largest denomination among African-American churches in the United States?

27. Who became the first African-American woman to command a U.S. Navy ship in 1989?

28. He launched the Black Power movement in 1966.

29. Huey Newton and this man founded the Black Panther Party in 1966.

30. Who was the first black lieutenant governor of Colorado, elected in 1974?

31. He became the first black Supreme Court justice in 1967.

21. New York City

22. Hazel R. O'Leary

23. Elijah Muhammed

24. Doris A. Daniels

25. Malcolm X

26. National Baptist Convention

27. Evelyn Fields

28. Stokely Carmichael

29. Bobby Seale

30. George L. Brown

31. Thurgood Marshall

32. This free black inventor became one of the richest men in Philadelphia and helped finance William Lloyd Garrison's *Liberator.*

33. Who was the first black astronaut?

34. He became the first black mayor of a major U.S. city in 1967.

35. He became the first black Secretary of the Army in 1977.

36. He resigned as the United Nations Ambassador after an unauthorized meeting with representatives of the Palestinian Liberation Organization in 1979.

37. Who was the first African-American to head an embassy in Europe?

38. In 1920 he became the first black executive secretary of the NAACP.

39. Who was elected the first black director of the American Library Association in 1972?

40. He was the first black governor of the Federal Reserve Board in 1966.

41. Who was the first African American to co-chair a national political convention?

32. James Forten

33. Robert H. Lawrence Jr.

34. Carl B. Stokes

35. Clifford Alexander Jr.

36. Andrew Young

37. Clifton R. Wharton Sr.

38. James Weldon Johnson

39. Robert Wedgeworth

40. Andrew F. Brimmer

41. Yvonne Braithwaite Burke

42. She was the first African-American keynote speaker of a national political convention.

43. He became the first black physician in 1783.

44. He was the first black to graduate from a U.S. medical college.

45. This leader of the Tuskegee Methodist Church initiated the founding of Tuskegee Institute.

46. He became the first black to get his Ph.D. from Harvard for a dissertation on the African slave trade in the United States.

47. In what year was the United Negro College Fund established?

48. This black mathematician and astronomer published ten almanacs between 1792 and 1802.

49. Which black writer did Winston Churchhill quote with the words, "If we must die — let it be not like hogs . . ." in his famous World War II speech?

50. Alice Dunnigan, the first black woman correspondent for the White House, covered the campaign of what president?

51. In 1991 he became the 106th Supreme Court Justice.

42. Barbara Jordan
43. James Derham
44. James Hall
45. Lewis Adams
46. W. E. B. DuBois

47. 1944
48. Benjamin Banneker
49. Claude McKay
50. Harry S Truman
51. Clarence Thomas

52. In what year did Yale University decide to offer a B.A. in Afro-American studies?

53. What is the oldest African-American periodical, which celebrated its centennial in 1984?

54. In Jackson, Mississippi, a federal building was named after this dental surgeon, businessman, and former head of the NAACP.

55. The Birmingham, Alabama, Rotary Club admitted its first African-American member in what year?

56. What post did Samuel Pierce hold in 1984, when he was the highest-ranked minority member of President Ronald Reagan's cabinet?

57. She became the first African American to be crowned Miss USA in 1990.

58. This newspaper publisher and Spingarn Medalist was the first black American to chair the Board of Trustees at Morgan State University.

59. During the Carter Administration, she became the first black woman Secretary of HUD.

60. Which president appointed Andrew Young ambassador to the United Nations?

52. 1976
53. *Philadelphia Tribune*
54. A. H. McCoy
55. 1984
56. Secretary of HUD

57. Carole Gist
58. Carl Murphy
59. Patricia R. Harris
60. Jimmy Carter

61. This minister from Philadelphia was elected House Budget Committee chairman in 1986.

62. Having attended Colgate and Columbia Universities and served as a Baptist minister in Harlem, he started his tenure in the U.S. House of Representatives in 1944.

63. The author of *Notes of a Processed Brother*, he helped establish a bill of rights in 1969–70 for New York City public high school students.

64. A scientist and brother of Howard University President Emeritus James Nabrit, he became the first black to receive a Ph.D. from Brown University in 1932.

65. In addition to owning and editing the *California Eagle*, a Los Angeles newspaper, she was the U.S. vice-presidential candidate for the Progressive Party in 1948.

66. What U.S. congresswoman attempted to win the Democratic Party presidential nomination in 1972?

67. Theodore Berry was elected mayor of this city in 1972.

68. In 1965 it became the first state to pass a racial imbalance law, which defined schools having 50 percent nonwhites as racially imbalanced.

61. William H. Gray III

62. Adam Clayton Powell Jr.

63. Donald Reeves

64. Samuel Nabrit

65. Carlotta A. Bass

66. Shirley Chisholm

67. Cincinnati, Ohio

68. Massachusetts

69. What was the first organization to set as its goal the formation of a separate nation for blacks in the United States?

70. What black congressman successfully fought for the commemoration of African-American women in a series of postage stamps?

71. Issued by the African Methodist Episcopal Church, it is the oldest black church periodical existing today.

72. What black sorority, established at Howard University in 1908, has chapters in 46 states and publishes *Ivy Leaf Magazine*?

73. Founded at Cornell in 1906, it is the oldest black fraternity in the nation.

74. This fraternal order consists of Nobles and Daughters of Isis, and focuses its charitable efforts on combating drug abuse and diseases that strike blacks.

75. Consisting of the blacks in the U.S. House of Representatives, this organization was founded in 1970.

76. At what college was Delta Sigma Theta Sorority, Inc., founded in 1913?

77. What major U.S. organization runs the ACT-SO Program (Afro-Academic, Cultural, Technological and Scientific Olympics), which awards scholarships to blacks?

69. The Black Muslims

70. Joseph Addabbo

71. *Christian Recorder*

72. Alpha Kappa Alpha Sorority

73. Alpha Phi Alpha Fraternity, Inc.

74. Ancient Egyptian Arabic Order Nobles Mystic Shrine, Inc. (AEAONMS)

75. Congressional Black Caucus

76. Howard University

77. The NAACP

78. In what New York City museum does the National Coalition of 100 Black Women hold its annual awards ceremony?

79. What organization publishes *The State of Black America* each year?

80. Which European nation was the first to stop trading African slaves to the United States in 1794?

81. The former director of the Southern Christian Leadership Conference, he was appointed special assistant on Urban Affairs to Governor Nelson Rockefeller.

82. He was 65 when he became the first black injured in the Civil War.

83. Who was the first black woman principal of a New York City public school?

84. What New York paper did Timothy Thomas Fortune found in 1883?

85. An editor of the *Memphis Free Speech*, she crusaded against lynching in the South around the turn of the century.

86. What distinguished educational administrator earned a Ph.D. from the Sorbonne in 1922 at the age of 66, and lived to be 105 years old?

78. Metropolitan Museum of Art

79. National Urban League

80. France

81. Wyatt Tee Walker

82. Nicolas Biddle

83. Gertrude Elise Ayer

84. *New York Freeman*

85. Ida B. Wells Barnett

86. Anna Julia Cooper

87. Dorothy B. Ferebee succeeded Mary McLeod Bethune as president of this organization.

88. Author of *The Negro Woman's College Education*, she was named "one of the 100 most influential Negroes of the Emancipation Centennial Year" by *Ebony* magazine in 1963.

89. The U.S. Supreme Court ordered the desegregation of what state's prisons in 1968?

90. In what year was the National Association of Black Journalists organized?

91. Who succeeded Dr. Martin Luther King Jr. as head of the Southern Christian Leadership Conference?

92. An executive with the United Church of Christ, he was one of the "Wilmington Ten," civil rights activists sentenced to 282 years in prison in 1972.

93. A U.S. district judge, he became Yale University's first African-American trustee in 1970.

94. In Washington, D.C., in 1970, he became the first black superintendent of schools in a major American city.

95. What is the formal name of the Black Muslims?

96. In what city was the major black newspaper, *Afro-American*, founded in 1892?

87. The National Council of Negro Women
88. Jeanne Noble
89. Alabama
90. 1976
91. Ralph D. Abernathy
92. Benjamin F. Chavers Jr.
93. A. Leon Higginbotham Jr.
94. Hugh H. Scott
95. The Lost-Found Nation of Islam in the Wilderness of North America
96. Baltimore

97. An attorney and Baptist minister, he was the first African American to serve on the Federal Communications Commission.

98. Who became the first black director of the American Library Association in 1972?

99. Assigned to Europe in 1972, this major general was the first black to command a U.S. Army division.

100. Whose 1972 promotion to major general made him the highest-ranking black officer in the U.S. Air Force?

101. In 1972 the Department of Housing and Urban Development guaranteed $14 million in land development bonds to this new town in North Carolina; it was the first such program sponsored by an African American.

102. In what year did the Order of the Elks admit blacks?

103. Started in 1973, it was the first black-owned and operated radio news network.

104. What civil rights activist was also the research chemist who isolated soya protein and held over 130 chemical patents?

105. The first private black medical college in the United States, it celebrated its 100th anniversary in 1976.

97. Benjamin L. Hooks
98. Robert Wedgeworth
99. Frederick E. Davidson
100. Daniel "Chappie" James
101. Soul City

102. 1973
103. National Black Network
104. Percy L. Julian
105. Meharry Medical College

106. What African-American educator, who is also a historian, psychologist, and scientist, cofounded an annual conference on infusing African and African-American content into traditional school curriculum?

107. What is the name of the slave who was the first to explore much of Arizona and New Mexico?

108. A trader who once was chief of the Crow Indians, he discovered Pueblo, Colorado, as well as a Sierra Nevada pass in California, which was named for him.

109. A plaque in Annapolis, Maryland, honors this black who took part in Admiral Robert E. Peary's expedition to the North Pole.

110. Elected mayor of Atlanta, Georgia, in 1973, he became the first black mayor of a major southeastern city.

111. He was considered the "recognized colored Republican leader" of New York City in the early twentieth century.

112. This church is the oldest African-American church in the North and was the largest U.S. Protestant church as well as a significant force in Harlem's history.

113. This Puerto Rican of African descent built one of the most important libraries devoted to African Americans.

106. Asa Hilliard III

107. Estevan(ico)

108. James P. Beckwourth

109. Matthew Henson

110. Maynard Jackson

111. Charles W. Anderson

112. Abyssinian Baptist Church

113. Arthur A. Schomburg

114. This politician became the first African American to be elected to the city council of New York.

115. A professor of philosophy at Howard University, he published *The New Negro* in 1925.

116. What was the new name given to the literary magazine *Negro Digest* after Hoyt Fuller revitalized it in 1970?

117. Liberated from slavery by Union soldiers in 1865, this poet from North Carolina published in the *Liberator*, the *North Star*, and the *Pennsylvania Gazette*.

118. Who was the first black real estate broker?

119. What was the first black college, established in 1837?

120. Having become the first black to command a U.S. Navy ship in 1966, he was appointed the first black admiral in the U.S. Navy in 1971.

121. She became the first black woman to graduate from a U.S. college when she received her degree from Oberlin College in 1862.

122. The first black to attend the University of North Carolina Law School, he was national chairman of CORE in 1963.

114. Adam Clayton Powell Jr.

115. Alain L. Locke

116. *Black World*

117. George Moses Horton

118. Henry M. Collins

119. Cheney State Training School

120. Samuel Lee Gravely Jr.

121. Mary Jane Patterson

122. Floyd B. McKissick

123. Who was the first black woman general, appointed on Sept. 1, 1979?

124. In 1966 she became the first black woman admitted to the Mississippi bar.

125. She was the first black woman to be elected president of the Girl Scouts of America in 1975.

126. Who was the first president of the Freedmen's Bank?

127. What U.S. Army sergeant developed an airframe center support, making greater rocket payloads possible by reducing deadweight?

128. Who was the first black president of the National Organization for Women?

129. She sat in the Chair of the Organization of Afro-American Unity in 1965 after the death of her brother, Malcolm X.

130. Who became the first woman Black Panther Party head in 1975?

131. What was the first black organization with a business orientation?

132. Who led a revolt of 1,000 slaves in Richmond, Virginia, in 1800?

123. Hazel Johnson

124. Marian Wright Edelman

125. Gloria Dean Scott

126. William A. Booth

127. Adolphus Samms

128. Aileen Hernandez

129. Ella Mae Collins

130. Elaine Brown

131. Free African Society

132. Gabriel Prosser

133. William Lloyd Garrison started this abolitionist newspaper in Boston in 1831.

134. In 1899 this dentist patented the first modern golf tee.

135. Who organized the Universal Negro Improvement Association?

136. What was the first all-black religious denomination in the United States?

137. His wooden clock was probably the first of its kind to be built in the United States.

138. His antislavery pamphlet, *Appeal*, incited white southerners to offer a reward for his capture in 1829.

139. He organized the Alabama Penny Savings Bank of Birmingham in 1890.

140. Where was the first black college founded?

141. With five blacks and seventeen whites, he led the attack on the United States arsenal at Harper's Ferry, Virginia, in 1859, to overthrow the slave powers.

142. Who was the first African American to practice law before the Supreme Court?

143. In what year was the first Fourteenth Amendment, which guaranteed citizenship to blacks, adopted?

133. Liberator

134. George F. Grant

135. Marcus Garvey

136. The African Methodist Episcopal Church (AME)

137. Benjamin Banneker

138. David Walker

139. W. R. Pettiford

140. Oxford, Pa.

141. John Brown

142. John S. Rock

143. 1868

144. Who founded the National Association of Colored Women?

145. In what year did the first Pan-African Congress meet?

146. This black-owned hotel was the leading hotel in Athens, Ohio, valued at $50,000 in 1883.

147. Established in 1893, it was the oldest industrial insurance company operated by blacks.

148. This black contractor invented a unique asphalt paving machine known as the Muller Paver.

149. Which black university was the first to receive a chapter of Phi Beta Kappa?

150. What African-American youth was brutally slain in Mississippi in 1955 for whistling at a white woman?

151. What 1964 act was responsible for such programs as Upward Bound, Head Start, and college work-study?

152. Who has been credited with drafting Alexander Graham Bell's telephone patents?

153. In what city was the Black Panther Party founded?

154. He discovered the method of preserving blood plasma, and organized the first blood bank during World War II.

155. In what year was the Fair Housing Act signed?

144. Mary Church Terrell
145. 1919
146. Hotel Berry
147. Southern Aid Society
148. John Muller
149. Fisk University
150. Emmett Till
151. The Economic Opportunity Act
152. Louis Howard Latimer
153. Oakland, Calif.
154. Charles R. Drew
155. 1968

156. Which black inventor has been issued the greatest number of U.S. patents?

157. How many black ambassadors did President Lyndon B. Johnson appoint?

158. When were black children first enrolled in all-white Mississippi public schools?

159. How many people were killed in the raid on Attica Prison?

160. When was the National Black Feminist Organization founded?

161. In what year did the Watts Riots occur?

162. In 1884 he patented a machine that made paper bags.

163. Along with Margaret Sloan, she founded the National Black Feminist Organization.

164. What organization's slogan is "A Mind is a Terrible Thing to Waste?"

165. Where is the birthplace of civil rights leader Medgar Evers?

166. Who is the first woman to argue a case before the U.S. Supreme Court in 1973?

156. Elijah McCoy

157. Five

158. 1970

159. 43

160. 1971

161. 1965

162. William B. Purvis

163. Eleanor Holmes Norton

164. The United Negro College Fund

165. Jackson, Miss.

166. Jewel LaFontant Mankarious

167. Once believed to be the country's richest man, he launched the Booker T. Washington Insurance Company

168. In what U.S. city can you find Scott Joplin's house?

169. Who is the founder of the nation's first and largest minority-owned insurance brokerage firm?

170. This woman cofounded the Alliance for Minority Opportunities.

171. This woman played a prominent role in the establishment of the National Baptist Convention.

172. This woman served as principal of an interracial school that educated children of Harvard faculty members just two decades after the slaves were freed.

173. She helped form the America-Women's Convention Auxiliary to the National Baptist Convention in 1900.

174. Who became the first woman president of the University of Houston?

175. His cosmetic product, "High-Brown Face Powder" made him the first African American to sell his products in Woolworth's, a mainstream outlet.

176. She was a spy for the Union Army during the Civil War.

167. A. G. Gaston

168. St. Louis

169. Ernesta Procope

170. Terrain Barnes-Bryant

171. Mary Cook

172. Maria Louise Baldwin

173. Nannie Helen Burroughs

174. Marguerite Ross Barnett

175. Anthony Overton

176. Elizabeth Bowser

177. Reginald Lewis founded this international food company in 1987 that became the largest black-owned business in the United States.

178. In 1925 she became the fourth black woman in the United States to earn a Ph.D. after attending the Sorbonne in Paris.

179. This university in the nation's capital was founded after the Civil War primarily to allow recently freed slaves to participate in post secondary education.

180. She was the first black woman officer to be commissioned in the Women's Army Auxiliary.

181. This women's federation began its fight for children's causes in 1908.

182. In what year did Crystal Bird Fauset become the first black woman to be elected to the Pennsylvania House of Representatives?

183. This pioneer in feminism during the nineteenth century said, "Let every female heart become united."

184. Who was the first black woman physician licensed to practice medicine in Georgia?

185. She was the first woman to become bishop of an Episcopal Church, elected in 1989.

---

177. TLC Beatrice International Holdings, Inc.

178. Anna Julia Cooper

179. Howard University

180. Charity Adams Early

181. Empire State Federation of Women's Clubs, Inc.

182. 1938

183. Maria W. Stewart

184. Eliza Anna Grier

185. Barbara Harris

186. Who was the third black woman to receive a Ph.D. in mathematics?

187. This organization succeeded in its efforts to support the professional black community in the 1930s.

188. Who said, "My girls and women, you should live that the world be a better place by your having lived in it?"

189. In 1992, as mission specialist on the space shuttle *Endeavor,* she became the first black woman to go into space.

190. Who founded the Lincoln Settlement House?

191. A vice president of a large utility, she became Washington D.C.'s first native-born and woman mayor.

192. This mathematician was inducted into the Ohio Women's Hall of Fame in 1989.

193. Who founded the National Coalition of 100 Black Women?

194. In 1985 she was elected the NAACP's first black woman president.

195. What is the most prominent vocation of black women since colonial times?

---

186. Gloria Hewitt

187. Housewives' League of Detroit

188. Clara A. Howard

189. Mae C. Jamison

190. Verina Morton

191. Sharon Pratt Kelly

192. Carolyn R. Mahoney

193. Jewell McCabe

194. Enolia McMillian

195. health care

196. On what date did Anne Moody participate in the controversial Jackson, Mississippi, lunch counter sit-in?

197. At what prominent nightclub in 1948 was Mollie Moon responsible for breaking the color line?

198. An attorney for the NAACP, she tried some of the twentieth century's most important civil rights cases.

199. She significantly improved the conditions at the St. Louis Children's Hospital.

200. This is the first site in North Carolina to honor a woman or an African American.

201. Who protested Oberlin College's segregation law in 1913?

202. She lifted the color ban for black nurses in the U.S. Army.

203. This abolitionist wanted the quote, "She was a friend of John Brown's" carved on her tombstone.

204. She was the first black woman to earn a Ph.D. in political science.

205. A civil rights activist and professor of English at Alabama State College, she was a prominent figure in the Montgomery bus boycott of 1955–56.

196. March 23, 1963

197. Rockefeller Center's Rainbow Room

198. Constance Baker Motley

199. Helen Nash

200. Charlotte Hawkins Brown Memorial

201. Mary Church Terrell

202. Estelle Massey

203. Mary Ellen Pleasant

204. Jewel Prestage

205. Jo Ann Robinson

206. What is the name of the first order of black nuns founded by the Haitian refugee Elizabeth Lange in 1829?

207. He was the first black man in the United States to earn a Ph.D. in physics.

208. An activist in more than 50 social reform organizations, including preparing the first case to be heard by the Supreme Court, she said, "I cannot be bought, and I will not be sold."

209. This principal of Hawaiian schools became a prominent figure in education.

210. This Underground Railroad conductor personally rescued 200 slaves.

211. Victoria Matthews founded this house for black women who migrated from the South.

212. In 1893 Fannie Barrier Williams gained fame at this event after speaking about the inequalities black women faced.

213. This canteen was built for black soldiers during World War II.

214. Black women fought adamantly for their rights in this world celebration of 1893.

215. She was a New Orleans business leader in the early 1900s.

206. Oblate Sisters of Providence
207. Edward A. Bouchet
208. Modjeska Simkins
209. Carlotta Stewart-Lai
210. Harriet Tubman

211. White Rose Mission
212. Chicago's World Fair
213. Camp Upton Hostess House
214. World's Columbian Exposition
215. Gertrude Willis

216. Who is black America's best-known scientist?

217. She pioneered several advances in the field of chemotherapy.

218. This astronaut lost his life on the *Challenger* in 1986.

219. What was the first black-owned company to be traded on the New York Stock Exchange?

220. Her work with children through the order of St. Luke earned Maggie Lena Walker this title.

221. This prominent businessman's motto was "Find a need and fill it."

222. How many black-owned firms were operating nationwide by 1990?

223. For whose wedding did Anne Lowe design a gown in 1968?

224. He was the second black designer in the United States to win the Coty Awards in 1983.

225. Fashion designer Patrick Kelly was the first American to be voted into this French design group in 1988.

226. She became a multimillonaire in 1990 for developing cosmetics especially for black women.

216. George Washington Carver

217. Jane Wright

218. Ronald E. McNair

219. BET Holdings

220. Saint Luke Grandmother

221. A. G. Gaston

222. 400,000

223. Jacqueline Kennedy Onassis

224. Willi Smith

225. Chambre Syndicate

226. Barbara Walden

227. He was given the U.S. Army's highest title of Chairman of the U.S. Joint Chiefs of Staff in 1989 and presided over Operation Desert Storm.

228. Who was crowned Miss America in 1989?

229. He became the first black police commissioner in Texas.

230. He was appointed Archbishop of the Roman Catholic diocese in Atlanta, Georgia, in 1988.

231. He donated $20 million dollars to Spelman College in 1988.

232. President George Bush named this Republican the Chairman of the U.S. Commission on Civil Rights in 1990.

233. Protests by blacks in the 1960s resulted in the passage of this congressional legislation concerning First Amendment freedoms.

234. Who was the first U.S. black governor, elected in Virginia?

235. What was the first black commercial bank, which opened in Harlem?

236. What year was the only one during which every state observed Martin Luther King Jr. Day?

227. Gen. Colin Powell

228. Debbye Turner

229. Lee P. Brown

230. Eugene Antonia Marino

231. Bill Cosby

232. Arthur Fletcher

233. Civil Rights Act of 1964

234. Douglas Wilder

235. Freedom National Bank

236. 1993

237. This Surgeon General endorsed sex education for all grade levels in 1993.

238. The headquarters of this radical black group in Philadelphia was destroyed by a police bomb in 1985.

239. She became the U.S. Army's first black female brigadier general in 1985.

240. Who became Baltimore's first black mayor?

241. In 1987 this prominent justice rated President Reagan as the president with the worst civil rights record.

242. President George Bush vetoed this bill, claiming it would "introduce the destructive force of quotas."

243. In 1991 President George Bush presented him with the Medal of Freedom for providing job opportunities to blacks in the United States and Africa.

244. In 1991 he became governor of Louisiana.

245. Inventor Frederick M. Jones won this award in 1991 for designing more than 60 devices to improve food product preservation.

246. The NAACP named him "Best Newscaster of the Year" for his reporting efforts during the Gulf War in 1991.

247. In 1993 this former pro football player became Minnesota's first black state Supreme Court Justice.

237. Joycelyn Elders

238. MOVE

239. Sherian Grace Cadoria

240. Kurt Schmoke

241. Thurgood Marshall

242. Civil Rights Bill of 1990

243. Leon Sullivan

244. Edwin A. Edwards

245. National Medal of Technology

246. Bernard Shaw

247. Alan Page

248. Described as "Teflon Mayor," he became the first black to lead a predominantly white city, Los Angeles, in 1973.

249. He was the first black to pass Florida's bar exam.

250. Who was the first black congresswoman from the "Deep South"?

251. Who was the first African American to become a four-star Army general?

252. This street in Atlanta, Georgia, is named the "Mecca of the modern civil rights movement."

253. Martin Luther King Jr. was pastor of this church in the 1950s.

254. In what Alabama city can you find the George Washington Carver Museum?

255. This museum in Mississippi honors black musicians' contributions to U.S. history.

256. Who was the president of the first black bank?

257. The fourth black female general in the U.S. Air Force, she earned her rank in 1990.

258. Which ground technician shot down the first scud missile in the Gulf War?

248. Tom Bradley

249. James Weldon Johnson

250. Barbara Jordan

251. Roscoe Robinson Jr.

252. Auburn Avenue

253. Dexter Avenue King
    Memorial Baptist Church

254. Tuskegee

255. Delta Blues Museum

256. John Roy Lynch

257. Marcelite J. Harris

258. Phoebe Jeter

259. She is a pioneer for successful drug-addiction treatment.

260. Who was he first black woman president of the National Medical Association in 1985?

261. She was the first black woman admitted to the American College of Surgeons.

262. She was the first black woman to lead a major city's public school system, in Washington, D.C.

263. What colony outlawed black slave importation until 1750?

264. This evangelist was hailed "the singing pilgrim" for her efforts in social and religious reform for blacks.

265. Ida Van Smith was inducted into this organization for her contributions to aviation in 1984.

266. Architect Jack Travis is noted for writing this "major book on black architecture."

267. What commission was developed as part of the Civil Rights Act of 1991?

268. In what year did the Congressional Black Caucus gain national recognition by meeting with President Richard Nixon?

269. Who is the longest serving black woman in Congress?

259. Muriel Petioni

260. Edith Irby Jones

261. Helen O. Dickens

262. Barbara Sizemore

263. Georgia

264. Amanda Berry Smith

265. International Forest of Friendship

266. *African American Architects: In Current Practice*

267. Glass Ceiling Commission

268. 1971

269. Rep. Cardiss Collins of Chicago

270. Who is the first congressman to represent Florida's District 23 after being removed from his judgeship?

271. She was the first black woman ever to hold office in Chicago within the Cook County government?

272. This congressman wrote the low income housing tax credit legislation that provides the majority of affordable housing in the United States.

273. Who is the first and only black person from Tennessee to ever be elected to Congress?

274. Who was the first black person to serve as Deputy Borough President in Brooklyn?

275. What congressman did the *Wall Street Journal* hail as "political star for the year 2000?"

276. One of the first black leaders to address HIV/AIDS issues, this congresswoman told the media "I don't have time to be polite."

277. In 1987 he became the youngest state senator in Louisiana and U.S. history.

278. The *National Law Journal* named him "Lawyer of the Year" in 1996.

279. Which gallery in the United States is considered to possess the finest collection of African-American art?

---

270. Alcee L. Hastings

271. Carol Moseley-Braun

272. Charles Rangel

273. Harold Eugene Ford

274. Edolphus Towns

275. Alan Wheat

276. Maxine Waters

277. Cleo Fields

278. Johnnie Cochran

279. The National Museum of American Art

280. What is the South's oldest black university?

281. In what year was the First National Black Theatre founded?

282. Who founded the first black female club in the state of Illinois?

283. She devoted 43 years to establishing the Moorland-Springarn Research Center at Howard University, one of the most important collections of written work on the African Diaspora.

284. She was the first black woman to join the Pennsylvania Supreme Court.

285. Who was the first nun to lead a U.S. parish?

286. What 1967 U.S. Supreme Court case found unconstitutional laws in 16 states that prohibited interracial marriages?

287. In what year was the National Women's Political Caucus established?

288. Lyndon B. Johnson awarded this opera singer the Medal of Freedom in 1963 for her role in supporting freedom and democracy.

289. In what year was the National Negro Labor Council established?

280. Shaw University

281. 1989

282. Ida Wells-Barnett

283. Dorothy Porter Wesley

284. Juanita Kidd Stout

285. Sister Cora Billings

286. *Loving v. Virginia*

287. 1971

288. Marian Anderson

289. 1951

290. In what year did Tuskegee Institute found a midwifery school ?

291. This organization, stressing black workers' rights, was established in 1936.

292. Who is the first woman to earn a doctorate in botany?

293. At age 19 she established the Palmer Memorial Institute, a school in rural North Carolina, where she educated countless students before retiring 50 years later.

294. She is considered the NAACP's first field worker.

295. One of the nation's most knowledgable librarians, and an expert on black life and culture, she was made curator of New York City's Schomburg Center for Research on black culture.

296. In what year was Howard University founded?

297. She is believed to have been Thomas Jefferson's mistress.

298. She built one of the United States's largest black history and literature collections, housed in the Chicago Public Library.

299. Who became the first African-American woman to head a law school, later becoming U.S. Secretary of Housing and Urban Development?

290. 1939

291. National Negro Congress

292. Jessie Jarue Mark

293. Charlotte Hawkins Brown

294. Kathryn Jackson

295. Jean Blackwell Hutson

296. 1867

297. Sally Hemings

298. Vivian G. Harsh

299. Patricia Roberts Harris

300. She posed as a man in the Continental Army for more than one year.

301. At her funeral, she was remembered as the "historian who never wrote."

302. Patricia A. French established this lucrative Parisian cosmetic company in 1983.

303. This black parent's group sported 187 chapters nationwide on its fiftieth anniversary in 1988.

304. President Ronald Reagan acknowledged her as an American hero in his 1985 State of the Union address.

305. The Medical Alumni Association named her a "living legend" in 1984.

306. This anthropologist, who studied race and gender issues, became the first black woman president at Spelman College in 1987.

307. This great choreographer's Ph.D. thesis on Haitian dances was published in three languages.

308. This pilot made her claim to fame as a barnstormer in the 1920s.

309. Septima Poinsette Clark received this highest award of South Carolina in 1982 for her work as a political activist and citizenship advocate.

300. Deborah Simpson

301. Vivian G. Harsh

302. Gazelle International

303. Jack and Jill

304. Clara "Mother Hale"

305. Lena Frances Edwards

306. Johnnetta Cole

307. Katherine Dunham

308. Bessie Coleman

309. Order of the Palmetto

310. Who established the Women's Political Council?

311. As a former employee, Anita Hill accused this judge of sexual misconduct in 1991 before the U.S. Senate Judiciary Commission.

312. What businesswoman at the turn of the century said, "I got myself a start by giving myself a start?"

313. She worked for Elizabeth Vanlew, Richmond, Virginia's famous Union Army spy.

314. Four white policemen from Los Angeles were charged with the beating of this man in 1992.

315. In 1986 she was recognized as the Humanist of the Year for her work in family planning.

316. What Maryland State Senator said, "One day I'm going to vote and pay back the insult to my father?"

317. She fought to eliminate sexism against black women in the early 1900s.

318. She established the Tuskegee Women's Club in 1895.

319. She was influential for shaping black Catholic history in the United States.

320. This North Carolina black women's college is only one of two still existing in the United States today.

321. This pilot cofounded the National Airmen's Association of America.

---

310. Mary Fair Banks

311. Clarence Thomas

312. Madame C. J. Walker (Sarah McWilliams)

313. Mary Elizabeth Bowsh

314. Rodney King

315. Faye Wattleton

316. Verda Welcome

317. Fannie Barber Williams

318. Margaret Washington Murray

319. Anne Marie Becroft

320. Bennett College

321. Willa Brown

322. In 1925 she became the fourth African-American woman to earn a Ph.D.

323. In what two states did a 1925 government census report on agriculture indicate that black farmers outnumbered white farmers?

324. In what year did Verina Morton found the Lincoln Settlement House?

325. In what year did Nancy Leftenant become the first black member of the regular Nurse Corps?

326. She was a strong advocate for teaching domestic work to women.

327. What former slave organized the Refugees' Home Colony in Canada during the mid-1800s for resettlement of escaped U.S. slaves?

328. She was called Denver's "Baby Doctor."

329. Who was the first black woman editor of a mainstream U.S. newspaper?

330. In what year was the Association for Black Women Historians established?

331. In 1979 she was the first African-American woman to earn a doctorate in chemical engineering.

332. In what year was the National Black Feminist Organization established?

322. Anna Julia Cooper
323. South Carolina and Mississippi
324. 1908
325. 1948
326. Jane Edna Hunter

327. Henry Walton Bibb
328. Jane Wright
329. Pearl Stewart
330. 1979
331. Jenny Patrick
332. 1973

333. She is the first woman to become justice for the U.S. Marine Corps.

334. This educator and political activist was placed on the FBI's Most Wanted List in 1970 for aiding an attempted courtroom escape, only to be acquitted later.

335. How many people were injured in the 1965 Watts riots?

336. She became the first black woman to earn the papal honor Pro Ecclesia et Pontifice.

337. Which progressive and nationally acclaimed Chicago educator turned down offers from both President Ronald Reagan and President George Bush to become U.S. Secretary of Education?

338. President John Adams wrote in his diary about this lady who successfully sued for her freedom in the Massachusetts higher courts.

339. In 1973 she founded the Children's Defense Fund to lobby for children's rights.

340. She was the first woman and first African American to be placed on the ballot in all 50 states as a presidential candidate in 1988.

341. The first African American elected to the U.S. Senate from the Democratic Party, she is also the first black woman U.S. Senator.

333. Sara J. Harper

334. Angela Davis

335. 900

336. Eleanora Figaro

337. Marva Collins

338. Jenny Slew

339. Marian Wright Edelman

340. Lenora Fulani

341. Carole Moseley Braun

342. Martin Luther King Jr. and his ministers broke from the National Baptist Convention in the early 1960s over his level of social activism and formed a new denomination called?

343. Who was the founder of TransAfrica?

344. Born Isabella Baumfree, she became an itinerant preacher during the mid-1800s, on a mission to abolish slavery.

345. What was the name of the book written by explorer Matthew Alexander Henson in 1912?

346. What African-American educational movement was promoted by Molefi Asante, Asa Hilliard III, and Leonard Jeffries during the 1980s?

347. This company, worth $2.1 billion, was at the top of the *Black Enterprise* list of 100 black-owned businesses in 1996.

348. He became the Navy's first black four-star admiral in 1996.

349. In 1996 he became the first cabinet secretary to die in an overseas mission.

350. This fraternity was founded at Howard University in 1914.

351. This biologist served as Vice President of the American Zoologists in 1930.

342. Progressive National Baptist Convention

343. Randall S. Robinson

344. Sojourner Truth

345. A Negro at the North Pole

346. Afrocentric Education

347. TLC Beatrice International Holdings, Inc.

348. J. Paul Reason

349. Commerce Secretary Ronald H. Brown

350. Phi Beta Sigma

351. Ernest Just

352. In what year were buses integrated in Montgomery, Alabama?

353. A former U.N. ambassador, he chaired the Kellogg Foundation's National Task Force on African-American Men and Boys in 1996.

354. In 1996 his Georgia Representative helped designate Alabama's 54-mile route of the Bloody Sunday march as a national historic trail.

355. In what year was the Missouri Compromise ratified?

356. He received a patent for the fire extinguisher in 1872.

357. He became vice dean of Howard University's law department in the 1930s.

358. He became the first black astronaut to enter space in 1983.

359. He won the first Kentucky Derby in 1875.

360. This black college in Pennsylvania was founded in 1854.

361. This restaurant owner was the first African American to appear on the cover of *Mademoiselle*.

362. Former Speaker of the California legislature, he became mayor of San Francisco in 1996 at age 62.

352. 1956

353. Andrew Young

354. John Lewis

355. 1820

356. Thomas J. Martin

357. Charles Hamilton Houston

358. Guin S. Bluford Jr.

359. Oscar Lewis

360. Lincoln University

361. Barbara Smith

362. Willie Brown

363. The history of black America began when a ship carrying 20 blacks landed in what English colony?

364. This black cabinetmaker built a wooden automobile.

365. Who was the first black man to pilot a plane across the United States?

366. Who published the first African-American periodical?

367. Who was the first African American to head the country's largest municipal public welfare program in New York City?

368. He convened the first Pan-African Congress, the first world conference for blacks, in Paris in 1919.

369. He was the first black Rhodes Scholar in 1907.

370. In what year did the first African Americans arrive in America?

371. According to John Winthrop's *Journal* the first African slaves were brought to New England in what year?

372. In 1641 this colony became the first to recognize slavery as a legal institution.

373. At what U.S. Army base was the first all-black Officer Training School established during World War I?

374. Which colony became the first to pass laws forbidding marriage between black men and white women in 1664?

363. Jamestown, Va.

364. David Bunt

365. Thomas Cox Allen

366. David Ruggles

367. James Russell Dumpson

368. W. E. B. DuBois

369. Alain L. Locke

370. 1619

371. 1638

372. Massachusetts

373. Fort Dodge

374. Maryland

375. By what religious group was the first formal anti-slavery resolution adopted in 1688?

376. His New York City school, established in 1704, was one of the first for African Americans.

377. Blacks in 1830 could be forcibly deported out of town according to a new city ordinance in this small Ohio city.

378. In 1996 this white owner of the Cincinnati Reds gave up day-to-day control of the team for two years for making racist remarks.

379. The theme of this light-skinned black leader of the NAACP during the 1930s was "Now is the time."

380. In 1991 President George Bush presented the sisters of Corporal Freddie Stowers with his Medal of Honor, approved posthumously, for the heroism he displayed in what war?

381. On November 12, 1775, this general issued an order that forbade black enlistment in the army.

382. A section that denounced slavery was deleted from this document before its adoption in 1776.

383. The first African-American church was established in 1773 in this southern city.

384. What black worker designed a railroad car coupling device for which a New York railroad paid $50,000 in 1897?

---

375. The Society of Friends

376. Elias Neau

377. Portsmouth

378. Marge Schott

379. Walter F. White

380. World War I

381. George Washington

382. The Declaration of Independence

383. Silver Bluff, S.C.

384. Andrew J. Beard

385. In 1900 Booker T. Washington formed this business organization in Boston.

386. In 1990 this city was chastised for its state not honoring the birthday of Martin Luther King Jr. through cancellations of events scheduled there by the International Association of Insurance Fraud Agencies, the National League of Cities, and the National Football League.

387. The first abolitionist society was established in this city in 1775.

388. The Continental Congress prohibited slavery in this part of the country in 1787.

389. He was the member of the commission that surveyed the District of Columbia in 1791.

390. Name the first bank operated for blacks in 1805.

391. In what year was the American Insurance Company of Philadelphia, the first managed by blacks, established?

392. Who led the slave conspiracy involving thousands of blacks in Charleston, South Carolina, and surrounding areas?

393. Considered the first black to receive a degree from an American college, he graduated from Middlebury College in 1823.

394. What was the name of the first black newspaper, published in 1827?

385. The National Negro Business League

386. Phoenix

387. Philadelphia

388. The Northwest Territory

389. Benjamin Banneker

390. The Freedman's Savings Bank

391. 1810

392. Denmark Vesey

393. Alexander Lucius Twilight

394. *Freedom's Journal*

395. He was the first black Roman Catholic bishop in the United States.

396. This black associate of Thomas Alva Edison drafted plans for the first electric street light.

397. Buried in Arlington National Cemetery next to Admiral Robert E. Peary, this African American was the first person to reach the North Pole.

398. By what name was black inventor Andrew J. Beard's railroad car coupling device popularly known?

399. Who was elected president of the first national black convention held in Philadelphia?

400. Who led the slave rebellion in Southampton County, Virginia, on August 21 to 23, 1831, in which 60 whites were killed?

401. How many African-American newspapers were published before the Civil War?

402. What was the name of the first antislavery political party, organized in 1839?

403. In 1957 under court-ordered integration, she attempted to enter the all-white Central High School in Little Rock, Arkansas, alone but was turned away.

404. H. C. Haynes of Chicago invented this barbershop item.

395. James Augustine Healy

396. Louis Howard Latimer

397. Matthew A. Henson

398. "Jenny Coupler"

399. Richard Allen

400. Nat Turner

401. 40

402. The Liberty Party

403. Elizabeth Eckford

404. The Haynes Razor Strop

405. Who was the first black to serve a full term in the United States Senate?

406. He was the first black lawyer admitted to the bar in 1945.

407. She escaped from slavery in 1849 and made 19 trips back to the South to rescue more than 300 slaves.

408. Inventions for automatically lubricating railroad cars were not considered authentic unless stamped with what slang expression denoting authenticity?

409. In 1913 he started the Standard Life Insurance Company of Atlanta.

410. Who published *Services of Colored Americans in the Wars of 1776 and 1812*, the first extended history of black Americans?

411. He published *The Constitution, Elevaton, Emigration, and Destiny of the Colored People of the United States*, the first major statement of the black nationalist position.

412. What 1857 U.S. Supreme Court decision stated that blacks were not citizens?

413. Shelby J. Davidson invented this office device.

414. Who sold his patented shoe soling machine to the United Shoe Machinery Company of Boston in 1883?

405. Blanche Kelso Bruce

406. Macon B. Allen

407. Harriet Tubman

408. "The Real McCoy"

409. Herman Perry

410. William C. Nell

411. Martin R. Delany

412. The Dred Scott decision

413. An adding machine

414. Jan E. Matzelinger

415. What lieutenant governor of Louisiana was born a slave in 1826 in New Orleans, and operated an employment service for former slaves?

416. What act of Congress protected the slaves against all rebels in 1862?

417. Contrary to popular belief, this measure did *not* free all slaves.

418. During what recent year did the Federal Bureau of Investigation begin an investigation of the burning of more than 30 churches in the South?

419. He was the first black to win the Congressional Medal of Honor for the attack on Fort Wagner in Charleston, South Carolina, in 1863.

420. What was the name of the first black daily newspaper?

421. In what year did Congress pass the Thirteenth Amendment to the Constitution, abolishing slavery in the United States?

422. In 1937 whose pioneer study on sickle cell anemia was released?

423. Who was the first African American awarded a Ph.D. degree?

424. In what year was the first Civil Rights Act passed?

415. Oscar James Dunn

416. The Second Confiscation Act

417. The Emancipation Proclamation

418. 1996

419. William H. Carney

420. *The New Orleans Tribune*

421. 1865

422. William Warwick Cardozo

423. Patrick Francis Healy

424. 1866

425. On March 2, 1866, this became the first southern city to allow blacks to vote.

426. This organization, known for terrorizing blacks, held its first national meeting in Nashville in April 1887.

427. Who invented the gas mask and the first electric stoplight signal?

428. In what year was the Independence Bank of Chicago founded?

429. This Virgin Islander played a major role in the political struggle between the United States and Mexico over the possession of California.

430. Who became the first black state cabinet officer when he was installed as the secretary of the state of South Carolina?

431. Members of what profession in Selma, Alabama, were the first to march en masse to the board of registrars to register to vote in 1965?

432. He became the first black to hold a major judicial position when he was elected to the South Carolina Supreme Court in 1870.

433. He was the first black U.S. Senator.

425. Alexandria, Va.

426. The Ku Klux Klan

427. Garrett A. Morgan

428. 1964

429. William Alexander Leidesdorff

430. Francis L. Cardozo

431. Teaching

432. Johnathon Jasper Wright

433. Hiram R. Revels

434. This New Orleans machinist and engineer was responsible for inventing in 1945 a patented multi-effect vacuum evaporating process that revolutionized sugar refining methods.

435. She was the first African-American woman lawyer in 1872.

436. He was the first black student at the U.S. Naval Academy in 1872.

437. He became the first African American to head a predominantly white university when he was inaugurated as president of Georgetown University in 1874.

438. From what school did the first black to receive a Ph.D. degree from a U.S. university receive his degree in physics?

439. He was the first black graduate from West Point.

440. This university appealed in a 1996 ruling by the Fifth Circuit Court of Appeal, stating that racial diversity should not be a consideration in college admissions.

441. What college was established by Booker T. Washington in 1881?

434. Norbert Rillieux	*438.* Yale University
435. Charlotte E. Ray	*439.* Henry O. Flipper
436. John Henry Conyers	*440.* University of Texas
437. Patrick Francis Healy	*441.* Tuskegee Institute

442. This state began the modern segregation movement in 1881 with the introduction of the Jim Crow railroad car.

443. In 1884 he became the first black to chair a national political party when he was elected temporary chairman of the Republican party.

444. Name the first training school for black nurses located in Chicago.

445. This scientist developed early rockets for the U.S. government.

446. What did the C in Project C stand for, in reference to demonstrations planned by the Southern Christian Leadership Conference during the early 1960s?

447. What Supreme Court decision upheld the "separate but equal" doctrine and began the age of Jim Crow in 1896?

448. She became the first black woman to head a bank when named president of Saint Luke Bank and Trust Company in 1903 in Richmond, Virginia.

449. He was the first black member of the Federal Parole Board.

450. On one occasion, the city of New Orleans borrowed money from this wealthy African-American.

451. What civil rights organization was founded by 47 whites and six blacks in 1907?

442. Tennessee   *447. Plessy* v. *Ferguson*
443. John R. Lynch   *448.* Maggie L. Walker
444. Provident Hospital   *449.* Scovel Richardson
445. Joseph Blair   *450.* Thomy Lafon
446. Confrontation   *451.* The NAACP

452. Who was the first editor of *The Crisis*, the periodical of the NAACP?

453. What bacteriologist developed the test for syphilis?

454. What major black newspaper was founded by John Henry Murphy in 1892?

455. Who developed a device for registering calls and detecting unauthorized telephone use?

456. When did the great migration of blacks from the South to northern cities begin?

457. What did Madame C. J. Walker manufacture?

458. How many riots occurred during the "Red Summer" of 1919?

459. In what year were the first Doctor of Philosophy degrees awarded to African-American women?

460. Who organized the first Negro History Week?

461. What was the percentage of black males unemployed in 1937, at the height of the Great Depression?

462. He was the first black Democratic congressman.

463. In what year did the U.S. Supreme Court rule that states must provide equal education facilities for blacks?

---

452. W. E. B. DuBois

453. William A. Hinton

454. *Baltimore Afro-American*

455. Charles V. Richley

456. 1915

457. Cosmetics

458. 26

459. 1921

460. Carter G. Woodson

461. 26 percent

462. Arthur L. Mitchell

463. 1938

464. She became the first black woman judge in 1939.

465. What famous black chemist obtained more than 100 patents?

466. This black businessman and politician, who died in 1848, left a $1.5 million estate, the bulk of which came from his land on the American River, one site of the 1849 gold rush.

467. Who was the first African-American general in the United States?

468. This Chairman of the National Labor Relations Board was named among *Ebony*'s 100 Most Influential Black Americans in 1996.

469. One of the great orators of the 1960s civil rights movement, this African-American minister received a D in preaching at the Chicago Theological Seminary because he would not write out his sermons.

470. In what year was the first issue of *Ebony* magazine published?

471. Who was the first black graduate of the U.S. Naval Academy?

472. Which president ordered "equality of treatment and opportunity in the armed forces"?

464. Jane Matilda Bolin

465. Percy L. Julian

466. William A. Leidesdorff

467. Benjamin Oliver Davis Sr.

468. William B. Gould IV

469. Jesse Jackson

470. 1945

471. Wesley A. Brown

472. Harry S Truman

473. In what city was WERD, the first black-owned radio station, opened in 1949?

474. She was the first black ambassador in the U.S. delegation to the United Nations.

475. Which African American was touted as the "greatest electrician in the world" by the *Catholic Tribune* in 1888?

476. This civil rights leader was coeditor and copublisher of the *Boston Guardian.*

477. Voted funniest mayor in a television contest in 1996, this African American leads a major U.S. city that has only a ten percent black population.

478. In what Illinois city did a mob of 3,500 keep a black family from moving?

479. Tuskegee Institute reported this as the first year in 71 years during which no lynchings occurred in the United States.

480. This scientist holds more than 75 patents related to meat packing and food preservation.

481. Robert L. Vann founded and published this Pittsburgh periodical.

482. What landmark Supreme Court decision declared segregation in public schools unconstitutional in 1954?

483. Who was the first black general in the U.S. Air Force?

473. Atlanta, Ga.

474. Edith Sampson

475. Granville T. Woods

476. William Monroe Trotter

477. Norman Rice of Seattle

478. Cicero

479. 1952

480. Lloyd A. Hall

481. Pittsburgh Courier

482. Brown v. *Board of Education of Topeka*

483. Benjamin O. Davis Jr.

484. Which twentieth century U.S. President appointed so many African Americans as advisors that they were called his "Black Cabinet"?

485. In 1980 minority employees of what major U.S. newspaper won an out-of-court settlement of $685,000 for a six-year racial discrimination suit?

486. What University of Texas math professor is responsible for increasing the number of black math majors from 50 in 1989 to 150 by 1996?

487. At the outbreak of the Civil War, about how many million slaves were in the United States?

488. For what does SNCC stand?

489. In 1990 she became the first African-American woman mayor of a major U.S. city.

490. In 1885 he obtained Patent No. 315,368 for the "telegraphony," a device that receives and transmits Morse code or voice messages.

491. He was allowed to register at the University of Mississippi after government intervention in 1962.

492. Four black girls were killed when this Birmingham church was bombed in 1963.

493. This NAACP field secretary was assassinated in front of his home in Jackson, Mississippi, in 1963.

484. Franklin D. Roosevelt
485. *New York Times*
486. Philip Uri Treisman
487. Four
488. Student Non-Violent Coordinating Committee
489. Sharon Pratt Kelley
490. Granville T. Woods
491. James H. Meredith
492. Sixteenth Street Baptist Church
493. Medgar W. Evers

494. Who was the first African-American network television reporter, hired by ABC-TV in 1962?

495. Who compiled a four-volume source of inventions by African Americans while serving as assistant examiner in the U.S. Patent Office?

496. What black inventor's shoe soling machine was known as "The Lasting Machine"?

497. Who introduced horseracing to California on his 35,000-acre tract of land on the American River?

498. Who was the sole dissenter among the U.S. Supreme Court justices in *Plessy* v. *Ferguson* in 1896, who said that the Constitution must be "color-blind"?

499. What was the first magazine to be edited by an African American?

500. She became the first African-American woman ambassador when appointed to Luxembourg in 1965.

501. J.W. Benton made the walk from his home in Kentucky to the Patent Office in Washington D.C., carrying a model of this invention.

502. Who has been the President of the Children's Defense Fund since its start in 1973?

503. Who was the first black woman federal judge?

494. Mal Goode

495. Henry E. Baker

496. Jan Matzelinger

497. William Alexander Leidesdorff

498. Justice John Marshall Harlan

499. The Mirror of Liberty

500. Patricia R. Harris

501. A derrick

502. Marian Wright Edelman

503. Constance Baker Motley

504. He patented a device for handling sails and later owned a sailmaking factory in Philadelphia.

505. Elected town clerk of Brownheim, Ohio, in the mid-1800s, this African-American lawyer became the first black ever elected to office in the United States.

506. What business and professional sorority for African Americans was founded in Detroit in 1943?

507. He was the first black sheriff in the South in the twentieth century.

508. What black nationalist leader received a pardon in 1927 from President Calvin Coolidge after serving two years of his sentence for mail fraud?

509. What department in the U.S. government in 1996 settled a bias suit by paying $3.8 million to black foreign service officers, who alleged they were not promoted because of their race?

510. Who was the first black child born in the English colonies in America?

511. Who was founder of the National Association of Market Developers?

512. In 1920 the Universal Negro Improvement Association approved what three colors for a new African-American flag?

504. James Forten
505. John Mercer Langston
506. Eta Phi Beta
507. Lucius D. Amerson
508. Marcus Garvey

509. Department of State
510. William Tucker
511. LeRoy W. Jeffries
512. Red, green, and black

513. She was the first woman in the history of Harvard University to receive a B.S. degree in chemical engineering.

514. In 1968, she founded National Domestics, a pioneer group that attempted to organize household workers.

515. Who was the first black member of the New York Stock Exchange?

516. Who was the first woman to chair the NAACP?

517. Who was the first African American nominated for president by a major national party in 1968?

518. Who was the first black woman elected to Congress?

519. In 1930 at the age of 24, this African-American inventor was teaching applied mathematics at L'Ecole Centrale in Paris.

520. Who is recognized by *Ebony* magazine as "the first Negro capitalist"?

521. What Democratic Representative from Maryland convened the First National Black Economic Summit in Baltimore?

522. In the first census held in 1790, what percent of the U.S. population consisted of African Americans?

513. Yvonne Clark

514. Dorothy Bolden

515. Joseph Searles III

516. Margaret Bush Wilson

517. Channing E. Phillips

518. Shirley Chisholm

519. Norbert Rillieux

520. Anthony Johnson

521. Parren Mitchell

522. 19.3 percent

523. What U.S. President established the Office of Minority Affairs?

524. According to 1995 Census Bureau reports, how many African Americans live in the United States?

525. The first record of freed slaves in New England is in 1646 when Governor Theophilus Eaton of what colony frees his slaves?

526. Who is the president and chief executive officer of the Martin Luther King Jr. Center for Nonviolent Social Change?

527. He was the first black to head a major agency of the U.S. government, as administrator of the Housing and Home Finance Agency.

528. Who became the first black diplomat to receive a major government appointment when named minister to Haiti in 1869?

529. In 1696 the Society of Friends threaten to expel Quakers from what colony because of their importation of slaves?

530. In what year did the African Methodist Episcopal Church authorize the ordination of women?

531. What early twentieth-century newspaper's motto was "A Newspaper Devoted Solely to the Interest of the Negro Race"?

523. Franklin D. Roosevelt

524. 33.5 million

525. Connecticut

526. Dexter King

527. Robert C. Weaver

528. Ebenezer Don Carlos Bassett

529. Pennsylvania

530. 1948

531. Negro World

532. He became the first black governor when Governor Warmoth of Louisiana was impeached in 1872.

533. What invention did James Smith, J. L. Pickering, W. G. Madison, and H. E. Hooker patent?

534. John Jones of Chicago made a million dollars at this occupation.

535. He became the first black physician in 1783.

536. In what field was 44 percent of the doctorate degrees awarded in 1995 to African Americans, according to the National Research Council?

537. Who was the first African American admitted to a medical society in 1854?

538. He was the first black inducted in Phi Beta Kappa in 1874.

539. Under what U.S. Army general were 90 percent of black soldiers in the Korean conflict serving in integrated units by 1953?

540. While at the U.S. Bureau of Standards, he invented a device used to test the durability of leather.

541. In what city did the Society for the Propagation of the Gospel in Foreign Parts in 1743 open a Christian missionary training school for blacks?

532. P. B. S. Pinchback

533. Airships

534. Tailoring

535. James Derham

536. Education

537. John V. DeGrasse

538. Edward A. Bouchet

539. Lt. Gen. Matthew B. Ridgway

540. Thomas J. Carter

541. Charleston, S.C.

542. Because they gave the Black Power salute on the podium, what two U.S. athletes were suspended from the U.S. Olympic team after the 1968 Mexico City Summer Games?

543. In 1996 she was appointed to the California Supreme Court, the first African-American woman to serve.

544. What black Revolutionary soldier reportedly killed British Major John Pitcairn?

545. In 1995 this newspaper publisher was voted in as mayor of Savannah, Georgia, the first African-American to lead the city.

546. What black served as advisor to President Abraham Lincoln, and as Consul General to the Republic of Haiti under President Benjamin Harrison?

547. In 1970 this state's legislature ruled that any person with 1/32 "black blood" was an African American.

548. Who was elected mayor of Oakland, California, in 1977?

549. Best known for her autobiography, this former slave taught at Wilberforce Academy and founded the Contraband Relief Association in 1862.

542. Tommie Smith and John Carlos
543. Janice Rogers Brown
544. Peter Salem
545. Floyd Adams Jr.
546. Frederick Douglass
547. Louisiana
548. Lionel J. Wilson
549. Elizabeth Keckley

550. William Stanley Braithwaite joined the English faculty of this first graduate school for African Americans in 1930.

551. Who was the black Detroit medical doctor accused of murder who Clarence Darrow successfully defended in 1925?

552. Who was the first black elected to the Mississippi legislature in 1967?

553. What organization for economic and political action did the Reverend Jesse Jackson found in 1970?

554. In what city and in what year did Martin Luther King Jr. give his memorable "I Have a Dream" speech?

555. Who was the first black woman to be named editor of *the Harvard Law Review,* in 1982?

556. This brigadier general is the first female general in the Army National Guard.

557. The first black congresswoman in Indiana, she was nicknamed "the hoosier lady."

558. Dr. Will Herzfeld was the first African American to be elected bishop of what church in 1984?

559. Who was the first black mayor of Philadelphia, Pennsylvania?

550. Atlanta University

551. Ossian Sweet

552. Robert Clark

553. People United to Save Humanity (PUSH)

554. Washington, D.C. in 1963

555. Annette Gordon

556. Rosetta Y. Burke

557. Katie Hall

558. The Lutheran Church

559. Wilson Goode

560. Who was the first black to earn his first mate's license, in 1918, and the first black captain of a U.S. Merchant Marine ship, in 1942?

561. What is called by many as the first U.S. civil rights organization, founded in New York in 1898?

562. What U.S. president vetoed the Civil Rights Restoration Act that Congress overrode, overturning the 1984 *Grove City College* v. *Bell* decision of the Supreme Court, which limited the enforcement of the act?

563. *Black Man in Red Russia: A Memoir* relates his experiences as a foreign correspondent in the U.S.S.R. from 1932 to 1946.

564. What black woman officer was the chief of the Army Nurse Corps during the Persian Gulf crisis?

565. This woman law professor at the University of Pennsylvania founded Commonplace, a nonprofit organization that promotes public discussions of race and gender issues.

566. Who is the psychiatrist and educator who recently developed for urban schools a teaching model that creates a learning environment where students are committed and accountable for their own learning?

567. Who became the mayor of Chapel Hill, North Carolina, in 1968?

560. Hugh N. Mulzac

561. Afro-American Council

562. Ronald Reagan

563. Homer Smith

564. Clara L. Adams-Ender

565. Lani Guinier

566. James Comer

567. Howard N. Lee

568. What city did James H. McGee become mayor of in 1969?

569. She relates her experiences as a Vietnam war correspondent from 1966 to 1967 in her book, *Good Men Die.*

570. What African American became mayor of Richmond, California, in 1971?

571. Who was President Ronald Reagan's National Security Advisor, the first black to hold this post?

572. Who was the first black pilot to earn an Air Transport Pilot's license, in 1932?

573. Located in Ohio, it was one of the first two U.S. black universities founded in the mid-1800s.

574. In the landmark Supreme Court decision of 1938, what school was ordered to admit Lloyd Gaines?

575. In 1790 what was the sole city in the United States without slaves?

576. The first black mayor of Atlantic City, New Jersey, he is a former superintendent of schools.

577. Who became the first African-American president of the American Association of Retired Persons in 1996?

568. Dayton, Ohio

569. Philippa Schuyler

570. Nathaniel Bates

571. Colin Luther Powell

572. Charles Alfred "Chief" Anderson

573. Wilberforce University

574. University of Missouri Law School

575. Boston

576. James L. Usry

577. Margaret A. Dixon

578. This Boston agency was founded in 1963 to help gifted minority high school students to obtain quality educations.

579. What black medic received a Medal of Honor in 1967 from President Lyndon Johnson for his heroic acts during Operation Hump in South Vietnam?

580. Who was the only black four-star general in 1996?

581. One of only four female U.S. Army generals when she retired in 1990, she was the first woman that reached the highest rank through the military police rather than the nursing corps.

582. When was the all-black American Bridge Association founded?

583. What was the name of the slave of W. B. Travis, a senior Texan officer at the Battle of the Alamo, who survived the attack and reported the assault to other Texas troops?

584. His bakery employed a large number of freedmen during the Civil War.

585. What African-American educator is the Director and founder of the Center for Multicultural Education at the University of Washington in Seattle?

578. A Better Chance (ABC)

579. Lawrence Joel

580. Johnnie Edward Wilson

581. Sherian Grace Cadoria

582. 1933

583. Joe Travis

584. Oscar James Dunn

585. James A. Banks

586. Established in 1898, this African-American order publishes *Elk News*, a quarterly newsletter.

587. Who was the leader of the SCLC who wrote the Project C demonstration plans in the 1960s?

588. Who was West Point's first African-American graduate (1889) to succeed in military service?

589. This Minneapolis mayor was named among *Ebony*'s 100 Most Influential Black Americans in 1996.

590. In 1965 Vivian Malone was the first black graduate from this institution.

591. In New Orleans in 1965 he became the first African-American to be appointed bishop.

592. Whose speech at the March on Washington in 1963 was rewritten at the last minute because of its inflammatory language?

593. This historically all-black town in the Northeast, once a station on the Underground Railroad, was incorporated in 1926.

594. He is the author of *The Negro Revolt*, which won second prize for reportage at the first World Festival of Negro Arts in Dakar, Senegal, in 1966.

586. Improved Benevolent Protective Order of Elks of the World

587. Wyatt Tee Walker

588. Charles Young

589. Sharon S. Belton

590. University of Alabama

591. Very Rev. Harold R. Perry

592. John Lewis

593. Lawnside, New Jersey

594. Louis Lomax

595. A prominent member of the Communist party who was convicted of plotting the overthrow of the U.S. government in 1953, he died in Moscow in 1965.

596. What black laborer discovered the body of Charles A. Lindbergh's kidnapped son in 1932?

597. A *Pittsburgh Courier* reporter for over 40 years, he was the first African-American international news correspondent.

598. Who is considered the first black to have graduated from Bowdoin College in 1826?

599. He was 65 when he became the first black injured in the Civil War.

600. Who became the first black police officer to command a Harlem district in 1963?

601. Who was the first African-American to win the title of "Catholic Mother of the Year" in 1952?

602. What was the nickname for the all-black 332d Fighter Group of the U.S. Army Air Corps, which escorted Allied bombers through European airspace on 1,578 missions during World War II?

603. In 1932 *The Journal of Negro Education* begins publication at what university?

595. Pettis Perry
596. William J. Allen
597. Joel A. Rogers
598. John Russwurm
599. Nicolas Biddle

600. Lloyd Sealy
601. Ruth Hall Thomas
602. Tuskegee Airmen
603. Howard University

604. He started four black magazines: *Negro Digest, Ebony, Tan,* and *Jet.*

605. A lawyer, she was the first African-American Ph.D.

606. What historian offered the first course in African civilization at any U.S. university in 1922?

607. He was elected mayor of Newark, New Jersey, in 1970.

608. Her 1962 book, *The Long Shadow of Little Rock*, tells of her efforts in the struggle to integrate schools in the South.

609. Previously an associate director of the *Philadelphia Christian Banner*, she founded the National Training School for Women and Girls in 1909.

610. What did African-American troops call one another during the Vietnam War?

611. What noted African American was the first to be honored on a U.S. postage stamp, in the 1940 Famous Americans series?

612. Who became the first black woman to be appointed by the President to a U.S. judgeship, in 1962?

613. In his 1971 book, *When God Was Black*, he relates his experiences as a participant in Billy Graham's religious crusades.

---

604. John H. Johnson

605. Sadie T.M. Alexander

606. William Leo Hansberry

607. Kenneth Allen Gibson

608. Daisy Bates

609. Nannie Helen Burroughs

610. Blood

611. Booker T. Washington

612. Marjorie Lawson

613. Bob Harrison

614. What African American invented and patented an automatic water feeder, a thermostat-setting apparatus, a vacuum pump, and a vacuum heating system?

615. This founder of the Martin Luther King Jr. Center was named among *Ebony*'s 100 Most Influential Black Americans in 1996.

616. For his heroism during the Korean conflict, this African-American pilot was the first black to receive the U.S. Navy's Distinguished Flying Cross.

617. A 1969 strike of Charlestown, North Carolina, hospital workers evolved into a major civil rights movement that lasted 113 days and was led by this organization.

618. At the turn of the century, this New York newspaper editor coined the term "Afro-American."

619. What Howard University president served as an ambassador in the U.S. delegation to the United Nations in 1965?

620. What is the name of the fleet of steamships that Marcus Garvey established in 1919 to link Africa and the United States?

621. Who was the first black to become a professor at Harvard Medical School, in 1949?

614. David N. Croswait Jr.

615. Coretta Scott King

616. Jesse Brown

617. Southern Christian Leadership Conference (SCLC)

618. T. Thomas Fortune

619. James M. Nabrit Jr.

620. Black Star Line

621. William A. Hinton

622. What black organization encouraged enlistments for World War I with the call: "Up brother, our race is calling"?

623. In 1970 he became the first Southern black minister in the history of the United Methodist Church to lead an all-white congregation.

624. Project C was the name of the demonstrations planned in what southern city during the 1960s?

625. In what year was "Red Summer," a season of racial conflict when over one hundred died?

626. A navy destroyer escort has been named after this man, who was the first African-American aviator and the first black naval officer to be killed in the Korean War.

627. Who founded the Women's Political Association of Harlem, New York, in 1918, one of the first black organizations to promote birth control?

628. In 1972 Kerry Pourcain became the first black president of this university.

629. Who founded *the New York Sun,* a leading newspaper in New York City, in 1879?

630. This comedian, civil rights leader, former track star, and essayist published *Nigger: An Autobiography* in 1964.

---

622. The Central Committee of Negro College Men

623. Henry Jogner Jr.

624. Birmingham

625. 1919

626. Ensign Jesse Leroy Brown

627. Cyril Briggs

628. Louisiana State University

629. T. Thomas Fortune

630. Dick Gregory

631. Who was the African-American soldier who rowed General George Washington across the Delaware River in 1776 and fought against the Hessians in the Battle of Trenton?

632. What state east of the Mississippi is the first to give African-American women the right to vote, in 1913?

633. In what year did the National Negro Doll Company begin distributing black dolls?

634. Who is the founder of Frelinghuysen University in Washington, D.C., devoted to the adult education of African Americans?

635. Despite a 1792 discriminatory law against blacks in the new U.S. military, which of the country's armed forces began to enlist free blacks in the 1790s?

636. In what city does Local 208, a black musician's union become the first black union to incorporate into the American Federation of Musicians in 1902?

637. In 1974 he became the first African-American moderator of the Presbyterian Church.

638. What was considered the most militant black newspaper in the South at the turn of the century?

639. Who was the author of the 1914 *The Negro in American History?*

631. Oliver Cromwell

632. Illinois

633. 1911

634. Jesse Lawson

635. U.S. Navy

636. Chicago

637. Rev. Dr. Lawrence W. Bottoms

638. Independent

639. John W. Cromwell

640. Who was the first black president of the predominantly white United Church of Christ in 1976?

641. About how many African Americans served in the Revolutionary Army in the War of Independence against England?

642. During the nineteenth century, how many states had laws prohibiting interracial marriage?

643. What black theology student at Vanderbilt University trained other students in nonviolence and role-played confrontations in preparation for student sit-ins in 1959 in Nashville?

644. This minister of Birmingham's Bethel Baptist Church and founder of the Alabama Christian Movement for Human Rights invited Martin Luther King Jr. and the SCLC to his city to confront segregation head on.

645. Who was the founder of the Washington Conservatory of Music and School of Expression for African Americans in Washington, D.C., in 1903?

646. What was the 1917 U.S. Supreme Court case in which a Louisville, Kentucky, law was overturned that forbade blacks and whites from living in the same neighborhood block?

640. Rev. Dr. Joseph H. Evans   *644.* Fred Shuttlesworth

641. 5,000   *645.* Harriet Marshall

642. 38   *646. Buchanan* v. *Warley*

643. James Lawson

647. This organization, which later became the American Methodist Episcopal Church, was founded by Richard Allen and Absalom Jones in Philadelphia in 1877.

648. Located in Wisconsin and the oldest cement building in the United States, this museum used to be a station on the Underground Railway.

649. She became the first African-American woman to be special master of the U.S. Virgin Islands' District Court in 1996.

650. In Gary, Indiana, in 1967, he became the first African-American mayor of a major northern city.

651. What was the name of the group of about 50 black Seminoles who had fled to Mexico in the 1850s and were later hired as Indian fighters by the U.S. government?

652. The youngest of 20 in a sharecropping family, she founded the Mississippi Freedom Democratic Party.

653. What was the 1944 U.S. Supreme Court decision that struck down Texas's all-white primary election law?

654. Who wrote *Imperium and Imperio,* viewed as the first "Black Power" novel, in 1899?

647. Free African Society

648. The Milton House Museum

649. Darlene Grant

650. Richard G. Hatcher

651. Seminole Negro Indian Scouts

652. Fannie Lou Hamer

653. Smith v. *Allwright*

654. Sutton Griggs

655. What African American's likeness in the form of a bronze bust is the first to stand in the halls of the U.S. Congress?

656. Established in 1972, it is the oldest black newspaper chain in the United States.

657. What NAACP monthly did W. E. B. DuBois edit from 1911 to 1933?

658. What civil rights activist and intellectual was the chief strategist behind the 1963 March on Washington?

659. Who became the first African American Texas Ranger, in 1988?

660. What African American who sought refuge with the Sioux served as General George A. Custer's interpreter?

661. Earvin "Magic" Johnson resigned from the National Commission on AIDS because of what U.S. President's lack of commitment to its purposes?

662. What African American was on the first stamp released in the Black Heritage series in 1978?

663. What former Tennessean slave campaigned for former slaves to leave the South and come to Kansas to establish all-black homestead communities?

655. Martin Luther King Jr.   *660.* Isaiah Dorman
656. San Francisco Metro Group   *661.* George Bush
657. *The Crisis*   *662.* Harriet Tubman
658. Bayard Rustin   *663.* Benjamin "Pap" Singleton
659. Lee Roy Young

664. Of what occupation was Lonnie Smith who sued for the right to vote against Texas's all-white primary law?

665. Who acquired a patent on a gas heating furnace in 1919?

666. In what city was the African Methodist Episcopal Church's Union Seminary, a manual labor school, founded in 1845?

667. In 1929 who was the only black candy manufacturer in the United States?

668. She was the first black U.S. woman to receive a dental degree from the University of Michigan in 1887.

669. In what city did the first African-American real estate broker operate in 1849?

670. In what year did a black first start selling new cars?

671. What black cowboy was known as Deadwood Dick?

672. Who is Cleveland's mayor, named among *Ebony*'s 100 Most Influential Black Americans in 1996.

673. What was the first major daily newspaper to be published by African Americans in the twentieth century?

674. He was the first black elected to the board of the New York Stock Exchange in 1972.

---

664. Dentist

665. Alice Walker

666. Columbus, Ohio

667. Arthur Herndon

668. Ida Gray Nelson Rollins

669. Pittsburgh, Penn.

670. 1940

671. Nat Love

672. Michael R. White

673. *Atlanta World*

674. Jerome H. Holland

675. In 1848 what black husband-wife team impersonated a slaveholder and his slave and escaped from Georgia to the North?

676. He invented a guided missile device and the artificial heart stimulator control unit.

677. About what percent of black voters supported Jimmy Carter's election to the presidency in 1976?

678. Who was the first black mayor of Chicago, Illinois?

679. In 1893 he organized the Southern Aid and Insurance Company.

680. What African-American was the founder of the first mosque in the United States, the Moorish Science Temple in Newark, New Jersey, in 1913?

681. She was the first African American to attempt to desegregate the University of Alabama.

682. In what year did Connie Slaughter, the first black alumna of the University of Mississippi, graduate?

683. In what year was the Odd Fellows, a black fraternal organization, formed?

684. He specialized in heating and ventilating system engineering, and patented numerous related inventions.

675. Ellen and William Craft

676. Otis Boykin

677. 90 percent

678. Harold Washington

679. B. L. Jordan

680. Noble Drew Ali

681. Autherine Lucy

682. 1967

683. 1846

684. David N. Croswait Jr.

685. What black entrepreneur lobbied against Colorado's discriminatory laws and influenced the passage of a 1885 law making it illegal to deny African Americans access to hotels and restaurants?

686. In what political party's convention did blacks participate for the first time, in 1843?

687. He invented the car record player "autophonic."

688. In 1976 Jewell Plumber Cobb became the first black woman dean of what women's college?

689. In 1898 he started the National Benefit Life Insurance Company.

690. Of what all-black Oklahoma town is Redd Foxx named police chief in 1974?

691. What black physician performed the first successful heart operation at Chicago's Provident Hospital in 1893?

692. In 1823 this prominent Philadelphia sailmaker was worth $100,000.

693. Who was the first African American to practice as an accountant?

694. What organization founded the Roger Williams University in Nashville, Tennessee, in 1873?

685. Barney Ford

686. Liberty Party

687. Robert Cheesboro

688. Douglass College

689. W. W. Browne

690. Taft

691. Daniel Hale Williams

692. James Forten

693. Joseph Cassey

694. The American Baptist Home Mission Society

695. What black organization was formed in 1852 in California to protest a law outlawing African Americans from testifying in court?

696. Who was the first African-American state bank commissioner of Rhode Island?

697. In what city was a convent for black nuns founded in 1842 called the Convent of the Holy Family?

698. In 1881 he developed the standard system for refining sugar, as well as glue, gelatin and condensed milk.

699. He was known as "Father Divine" when he preached of a "heaven on earth" for blacks in the 1920s and 1930s.

700. What Virginia congressman is considered the "Father of Black Politics in America"?

701. The American Colonization Society tried to ease racial problems by sending free blacks to this nation.

702. What black Presbyterian minister and orator of the early nineteenth century was known as the "black Daniel Webster?

703. When installed as lieutenant Governor of Louisiana in 1868, he became the highest-ranked black elected official.

704. In what year did Harriet Tubman escape from slavery?

695. Franchise League

696. Nivelle Beaubien

697. New Orleans

698. Norbert Rillieux

699. George Baker

700. John Mercer Langston

701. Liberia

702. Samuel Ringgold Ward

703. Oscar James Dunn

704. 1849

705. Under what name was Lincoln University, an early black college, incorporated in 1842?

706. He claimed he was the richest black man in the United States in 1850.

707. In what year did Congress charter the Freedmen's Bank of Birmingham?

708. What Native American culture welcomed escaped slaves into their communities from 1750 to the 1840s in exchange for their support in fighting territorial claims against the U.S. government?

709. This Philadelphia African American entered the coal business in 1865, amassing a fortune.

710. He operated a successful grocery store in 1866 in Atlanta, Georgia, and accumulated $60,000.

711. What was the name of the real estate firm founded by a group of African-American men in Cincinnati in 1839?

712. Who organized the 1995 Million Man March on Washington, D.C.?

713. Passing as a white man, he became the first black to fight for the Union Army in 1861.

705. Ashman Institute
706. Martin R. Delaney
707. 1865
708. Seminole nation
709. William Still

710. James Tate
711. The Iron Chest Company
712. Louis Farrakhan
713. James Stone

714. In what city in 1837 did the Institute for Colored Youth, the first black traditional (nonvocational) high school, open?

715. What black company entered automobile manufacturing in 1900?

716. He owned the street railway system and Arkansas state fairgrounds in Pine Bluff in 1886.

717. Who was the first black graduate of a theological seminary, from Princeton Theological Seminary in 1825?

718. He was the first black mayor of Newport, Rhode Island.

719. He invented a smokeless device for cooking hickory-flavored meat.

720. One of North America's "mountain men," this African-American hunter served as an interpreter and guide to North American fur-trading companies.

721. What African-American woman wrote *The Negro in American Culture,* published in 1956?

722. Students from what four schools in Nashville trained in nonviolence in 1959 to prepare for sit-in protests against segregation?

723. Who founded Hale House in Harlem, New York, a home for substance-addicted and AIDS-infected babies?

724. When was the last all-black army unit, the 24th infantry, deactivated by Congress?

725. She founded the Richmond Hospital in Virginia.

726. What former trooper in the Ninth Cavalry Regiment was marshal in the formerly lawless gold-mining town of Yankee Hill, Colorado, from 1874–77?

727. In 1957 the Prayer Pilgrimage, organized by the NAACP, is held in the nation's capital by what government building?

728. Where is Spelman College located?

729. What eminent African-American sociologist wrote *Black Bourgeoisie*?

730. While working for Chicago's Glidden Corporation, Percy Julian extracted a soya protein used in developing the World War II fire extinguishers known by this name.

731. Once known as the "Dean of Negro Editors," this African-American Republican founded the *New York Age* in 1884.

732. What does SCLC stand for?

723. Clara Hale

724. 1951

725. Mary E. Burwell

726. Willie Kennard

727. Lincoln Memorial

728. Atlanta, Georgia

729. E. Franklin Frazier

730. Aero foam

731. Timothy Thomas Fortune

732. The Southern Christian Leadership Conference

733. Who first succeeded in making the drug cortisone widely marketable at a reasonable price?

734. This slave received no credit for his role in developing the McCormick Grain Harvester alongside his master, Cyrus McCormick.

735. He invented a two-dimensional slide rule.

736. What Alabama businessman posted Martin Luther King Jr.'s $5,000 bail when he was arrested in Birmingham for marching without a permit?

737. By whom was the largest black newspaper in 1897 edited?

738. In 1900 he owned a successful hotel in New York City worth $75,000.

739. Who became the first black certified public accountant in the United States?

740. What member of the slave crew of the Confederate ship, *Planter,* disguised himself and successfully sailed past Confederate forts and surrendered the boat to the Union forces?

741. Who was the first black doctor in the United States?

742. A. P. Albert, a Creole, invented a machine for picking this crop.

733. Percy Julian

734. Jo Anderson

735. Clarence Reed White

736. Arthur George Gaston

737. John Mitchell

738. John B. Nail

739. Jesse B. Blayton

740. Robert Smalls

741. James Derham

742. Cotton

743. What famous African American was the first to appear on a U.S. coin, a fifty-cent piece issued in 1946?

744. This African-American bishop was named in 1996 as the head of the Catholic Relief Services, the first black to lead the aid agency.

745. In 1966 he became the first African American elected to be a Senator in the U.S. Senate since Reconstruction.

746. Who was the woman president of the Arkansas NAACP who advised the "Little Rock Nine" about entering Central High School?

747. This African-American abolitionist also loathed gender discrimination and declined his seat at the 1840 World Anti-Slavery Conference because women delegates had been refused their seats.

748. Who invented the potato chip?

749. What U.S. president made more appointments of blacks to high level federal posts than any previous chief executive?

750. How many top level federal appointments did President Richard Nixon award to blacks?

751. What black Pullman car porter, active in Montgomery's local civil rights groups, posted bail for Rosa Parks in 1955?

743. Booker T. Washington

744. John H. Ricard

745. Edward W. Brooke

746. Daisy Bates

747. Charles Lenox Remond

748. Hyram S. Thomas

749. Lyndon B. Johnson

750. Three

751. E. D. Nixon

752. In what year did an African American first become a certified public accountant?

753. What was the name given to the African-American soldiers that fought in the government's wars against Native Americans and patrolled the West from 1865 to the early 1900s?

754. In what year did National Urban League executive, Whitney M. Young, die?

755. Who was the first black new automobile dealer in the United States?

756. By what name was Hyram Thomas's invention originally known?

757. When did the National Negro Finance Corporation begin?

758. Who was the first African American to be licensed to practice medicine in the United States?

759. This Philadelphia candymaker and confectioner is known as the "man who invented ice cream."

760. In what year were a black man and a white woman married legally for the first time in North Carolina?

761. What journalist was the first black to be elected to membership in the Gridiron Club, a prestigious organization of Washington newsmen?

752. 1928
753. Buffalo Soldiers
754. 1971
755. Edward Davis
756. Saratoga Chip

757. 1924
758. James Derham
759. Augustus Jackson
760. 1971
761. Carl T. Rowan

762. Author of *From the Outhouse to the White House,* she was the first African-American woman to work in the White House social office—during the Reagan administration.

763. He owned a toy store at age 12.

764. Who was the first black federal judge?

765. He wrote "Carry Me Back to Ole Virginny," the state song of Virginia.

766. Who was the first black Secretary of Commerce?

767. What was the name of the swamp on the border between North Carolina and Virginia in which dozens of runaway slaves successfully hid from their masters in the late 1700s and early 1800s?

768. What was the only Southern state to permit slave enlistments in the military in 1780?

769. Since 1996 the Black Panther Party archives, including legal documents, correspondence, and photographs, have been housed in what university's library?

770. He invented thermostatically controlled air devices.

771. He was elected president of the Borough of Manhattan in 1953, the highest municipal post for a black.

762. Bernyce Fletcher

763. Cephus Hauser

764. William H. Hastie

765. James A. Bland

766. Ronald H. Brown

767. Great Dismal Swamp

768. Maryland

769. Stanford UnIversity

770. Solomon Harper

771. Hulan Jack

772. In what state is Grambling State University located?

773. In what year was the Colored Merchants Association founded?

774. He conducted a study of African-American business enterprises in 1898.

775. Because of his work on this Apollo 16 instrument, George Carruthers was commended by NASA for outstanding scientific achievement.

776. In what city is Meharry Medical College located?

777. During the early 1800s this city was considered "the seat of black affluence."

778. He opened a restaurant in New York City where George Washington was a frequent guest and where the New York Chamber of Commerce was organized.

779. In what city is Morehouse College located?

780. Who was respected as the "elder statesman" among civil rights leaders during the mid-twentieth century?

781. He founded the Citizens Federal Savings and Loan Association and Booker T. Washington Insurance Co. Inc., of Birmingham, Alabama.

782. In what state is Tougaloo College located?

772. Louisiana
773. 1928
774. W. E. B. DuBois
775. ultraviolet camera/ spectograph
776. Nashville, Tennessee
777. Philadelphia
778. Samuel Fraunces
779. Atlanta, Georgia
780. A. Philip Randolph
781. A. G. Gaston
782. Mississippi

783. Who was the first black woman licensed pilot in the United States?

784. Who refused to patent any of his agricultural innovations saying, "God gave them to me, how can I sell them to someone else?"

785. What African-American educator, who was a Fulbright scholar in the early 1980s, became President of the National Association for Multicultural Education in 1993?

786. Written in 1923, this was the first published study of black banks.

787. Whom did Eleanor Roosevelt invite to the White House in defiance of her social critics?

788. Having shot down four enemy planes during the attack on Pearl Harbor, he received the Navy Cross.

789. What organization refused blood donations from African-Americans in 1941?

790. Name the first black-owned bank begun in 1888 in Richmond, Virginia.

791. He was issued a total of 61 patents, among them an air conditioning unit for field hospitals, a portable X-ray machine, and a refrigerator for military field kitchens.

783. Bessie Coleman

784. George Washington Carver

785. Carl A. Grant

786. *The Negro as Capitalist*

787. The National Council of Negro Women

788. Dorie Miller

789. The American Red Cross

790. The True Reformers Bank

791. Frederick McKinley Jones

792. Who was the Reverend Jesse Jackson Sr.'s campaign manager when he ran for U.S. President in 1988?

793. Where did CORE hold its first sit-in?

794. Who founded the Nation of Islam in 1934?

795. In 1964 FBI agents found buried bodies of three civil rights workers in what town?

796. Who was the first African-American professional nurse?

797. He helped develop the Belzer Kidney Perfusion Machine, crucial to the process of transplanting kidneys.

798. In what year did the first black-owned bank open?

799. W. Montague Cobb has been cited for his studies in what disciplines?

800. Who was the first black mayor of New Orleans, Louisiana?

801. After 1800, this African-American restaurateur opened an eating house near Wall Street.

802. What was the second bank organized and administered by blacks in 1888?

803. What historically all-black college published *The Bluefieldian?*

792. Ronald H. Brown
793. Chicago
794. W. D. Fard
795. Philadelphia, Mississippi
796. Mary Eliza Mahoney
797. Sidney L. Kauntz

798. 1888
799. anatomy and physical anthropology
800. Ernest Morial
801. Thomas Downing
802. Capital Savings Bank
803. West Virginia State College

804. What physician was the first to treat president James A. Garfield after he was shot?

805. What Boston African American had by 1880 established himself as the second largest merchant tailor in Massachusetts?

806. Who opened the first black-owned drugstore in the Southwest, in Waco, Texas, in 1890?

807. She became the first black chancellor of a predominantly white institution at the University of Colorado.

808. Who invented the Synchronous Multiple Railway Telegraph?

809. She was the first African-American couture designer, working for such names as Henri Bendel and Neiman Marcus.

810. She was the nation's first African-American woman prosecutor.

811. Who was the first black and first woman special judge for the Second Judicial District of Mississippi?

812. She became the first woman and the first black Assistant Secretary at the U.S. Department of Agriculture.

813. She was Mississippi's first African-American woman mayor.

804. Charles B. Purvis
805. J. H. Lewis
806. Monroe Majors
807. Mary Berry
808. Granville T. Woods
809. Anne Lowe
810. Anne Thompson
811. Constance Iona Slaughter
812. Joan S. Wallace
813. Unita Blackwell

814. Who was the first woman and the first black to head a State Department Bureau with the rank of assistant secretary?

815. She was the first black woman to receive an M.D. degree in 1870.

816. In what year did the New York Stock Exchange accept its first black member?

817. Who organized the National Association of Colored Graduate Nurses in 1908?

818. To whom did Garrett A. Morgan sell his 1923 patented automatic stoplight signal for $40,000?

819. This English professor at Brown University edited the first college guide for black students.

820. Who is the first African American to be elected president of the National League of Cities?

821. He organized in 1919 the Black Star Line of steamships.

822. This military regiment won the *Croix de Guerre* in World War I.

823. Name the African-American cowboy who "never missed anything" and was nicknamed Deadwood Dick.

814. Barbara Watson

815. Susan Smith McKinney Steward

816. 1970

817. Martha Franklin

818. General Electric

819. Barry Beckham

820. Carl B. Stokes

821. Marcus Garvey

822. 369th Colored Infantry

823. Nat Love

824. Chicago's black residents elected him to be the first African-American congressman since 1901 — and the first elected from the North.

825. Who was the first black mayor of Pasadena, California, and the first woman to serve as mayor of a U.S. city of 100,000 or more people?

826. She became the first woman to sit on the Federal Appeals Court in Manhattan in 1979.

827. How many death threats did the Rev. Jesse Jackson receive when he ran for president in 1984?

828. Professor of Law at Georgetown University, she was head of the Equal Employment Opportunity Commission in the Carter Administration.

829. He became Michigan's first African-American congressman.

830. In 1974 he became the first black state senator to serve in Alabama since Reconstruction.

831. He succeeded Andrew Young as chief U.S. delegate to the United Nations.

832. Who authored the eloquent defense of the African-American during slavery, *The Condition of . . . the Colored People in 1852*?

---

824. Oscar De Priest

825. Loretta Thompson Glickman

826. Amalya Lyle Kearse

827. 311

828. Eleanor Holmes Norton

829. Charles C. Diggs Jr.

830. U. W. Clemon

831. Donald F. McHenry

832. Martin R. Delaney

833. He was appointed president of the City University of New York in 1981.

834. This ex-slave introduced the idea of the Freedman's Memorial Monument for Abraham Lincoln in Washington, D.C., the day after Lincoln's assassination.

835. The first African-American graduate of Harvard College, he was dean of Howard University's Law School from 1879 to 1880.

836. He was the first black to serve in Ohio's state senate and became known as the "Daddy of Labor Day" for introducing the state's Labor Day bill.

837. From Ottumwa, Iowa, he was the first African American to be nominated for President of the United States in 1904.

838. President Dwight D. Eisenhower appointed him as the first black executive in the White House in 1955.

839. Who was the first black mayor of Detroit, Michigan?

840. He became the first black president of Fisk University in 1946.

841. Who was the first African American to serve as a full delegate to the United Nations?

842. She was the first president of the National Association of Colored Women.

833. Bernard Harleston

834. Charlotte Scott

835. Richard T. Greener

836. John P. Green

837. George Edwin Taylor

838. E. Frederic Morrow

839. Coleman Young

840. Charles S. Johnson

841. Charles H. Mahoney

842. Mary Church Terrell

843. She founded Bethune-Cookman College, the National Council of Negro Women, and was an advisor to President Franklin D. Roosevelt.

844. Who founded the United Negro College Fund while president of Tuskegee?

845. Executive secretary of the NAACP during the key World War II growth period, he traveled to the South to investigate lynchings of blacks because he could pass for white.

846. He told the Senate Armed Services Committee in 1948 that he would urge black youths to resist the draft unless discrimination was banned.

847. Who was the first black appointed to Federal District Court in the continental United States?

848. He became the first black congressman from the West when elected from Los Angeles in 1962.

849. He was promoted to four star general and commander-in-chief of the North American Air Defense Command in 1975.

850. Named president of the Ford Foundation in 1979, he was the first black to head a major foundation.

851. Who became the first black woman elected president of the Borough of Manhattan in 1965?

843. Mary McLeod Bethune

844. Frederick Patterson

845. Walter White

846. A. Philip Randolph

847. James B. Parsons

848. Augustus F. Hawkins

849. Gen. Daniel "Chappie" James

850. Franklin A. Thomas

851. Constance Baker Motley

852. This former aide to Martin Luther King Jr. became the first nonvoting congressional delegate from the District of Columbia since Reconstruction.

853. He headed the United Negro College Fund before his 1971 appointment as executive director of the National Urban League.

854. Name the first black state supreme court justice in the South of the twentieth century, appointed in 1975.

855. Who was the first black bishop of the Washington, D.C., Episcopal diocese?

856. She was the first black woman ambassador, to Luxembourg, in 1965.

857. This Chicago resident was posthumously awarded the Congressional Medal of Honor for bravery in Vietnam.

858. She was the first black president of the YWCA.

859. What position did Thurgood Marshall hold before being confirmed to the Supreme Court?

860. Who was the first black woman named deputy solicitor general in 1972?

861. The sit-in movement began in 1960 when four students from what college sat down at a lunch counter in Greensboro, N.C.?

852. Walter Fauntroy

853. Vernon E. Jordan

854. Joseph W. Hatchett

855. John T. Walker

856. Patricia Roberts Harris

857. Milton Olive Jr.

858. Helen Jackson Wilkins Claytor

859. U.S. Solicitor General

860. Jewel Lafontant

861. North Carolina A&T

862. She was publisher of the *Arkansas State Press* during the 1957 school integration crisis in Little Rock, Arkansas.

863. A Morehouse College president for 27 years, he became the first African-American president of the Atlanta Board of Education.

864. He became the first black to head a standing committee of Congress in 1949.

865. Name the associate press secretary to President John F. Kennedy.

866. The first black dean of the college of Brown University, he became president of Morehouse College in 1995.

867. Name the first African-American elected mayor of Pritchard, Alabama.

868. Who was the first black admiral in the U.S. Navy?

869. Who defeated Adam Clayton Powell in 1970, ending the career of one of black America's most powerful politicians?

870. This graduate of the Yale Law School was appointed commissioner and chairman of the U.S. Equal Employment Opportunity Commission by President Ronald Reagan in 1982.

---

862. Daisy Bates
863. Benjamin Mays
864. William L. Dawson
865. Andrew Hatcher
866. Walter Massey

867. A. J. Cooper
868. Samuel Lee Gravely Jr.
869. Charles Rangel
870. Clarence Thomas

871. Born in Trinidad, he was elected lieutenant governor of California in 1975 and to the House of Representatives in 1980.

872. A Morehouse College graduate, he is the only professional librarian in the House of Representatives.

873. He argued the landmark "stop and frisk" case of *Terry* v. *Ohio* in the United States Supreme Court in 1968.

874. This executive director of the United Negro College Fund was a legal officer with the Ford Foundation.

875. This judge authored the important study of race and the American legal process, *In the Matter of Color*.

876. He was elected superintendent of public instruction for California in 1970.

877. In 1971 he was the first black mayor in the history of Tuskegee, Alabama.

878. He helped found SNCC, was its national chairman in 1960, and became the second elected mayor of the District of Columbia in 1979.

879. Who developed Soul City, the prototype new town located in Warren County, North Carolina?

880. By the eighteenth century, this colony was the leader in the slave trade.

871. Mervyn M. Dymally

872. Major R. Owens

873. Louis Stokes

874. Christopher F. Edley

875. A. Leon Higginbotham Jr.

876. Wilson Riles

877. Johnny L. Ford

878. Marion S. Barry Jr.

879. Floyd B. McKissick

880. Rhode Island

881. President of the NAACP Legal Defense and Educational Fund, he argued the landmark *Swann* v. *Charlotte-Mecklenburg Board of Education,* resulting in crosstown busing.

882. Who became the first black member of Congress from Ohio in 1968?

883. Who in 1979 was named the first African-American general in the Marine Corps?

884. Name the first black woman president of the National Bar Association.

885. This journalist became the majority shareholder in the corporation that purchased the Oakland, California, *Tribune* newspaper in 1982.

886. Whose release did Rev. Jesse Jackson negotiate after this lieutenant was shot down over Lebanon in 1984?

881. Julius LeVonne Chambers   *884.* Arnette R. Hubbard
882. Louis Stokes   *885.* Robert C. Maynard
883. Frank E. Peterson Jr.   *886.* Robert O. Goodman Jr.

Art and Literature

887. Who was called "the poet laureate of the Negro race"?

888. What black landscape painter helped George Whitaker and Charles Stetson found the Providence Art Club in 1880?

889. From what city are the 17 poets who wrote *Les Cennelles*, the first anthology of African-American verse published in the United States in 1845?

890. Who was the editor and publisher of an illustrated fashion journal for black women, first released in 1981?

891. Carlene Hatcher Polite was one of the first black women writers to address turbulence in relationships between black men and women in this 1967 novel.

892. Having been encouraged by Thomas Eakins to paint genre scenes, he executed *The Banjo Lesson* in 1893.

887. W. E. B. DuBois

888. Edward Bannister

889. New Orleans

890. Julia Ringwood Coston

891. The Flagellants

892. Henry Ossawa Tanner

893. In 1990 the Mystery Writers of America nominated this novel, written by Walter Mosley, as best of the year.

894. Richmond Barthe's subject for this full-figure sculpture was Rose McClendon's portrayal of Serena in *Porgy*.

895. His 1760 poem, "An Evening Thought: Salvation by Christ and Penitential Cries," is the earliest known work published by an African American.

896. Charles Waddell Chestnutt, a turn-of-the century author renowned for his short stories, published a biography of what famous African American?

897. What 1874 book by a former slave reached its eighth edition in London only five years after publication?

898. After he had published his *Appeal* in 1829, a reward of $10,000 was placed on his head.

899. What is Langston Hughes's first autobiography called?

900. For what 1927 work is James Weldon Johnson well known?

901. Jean Toomer published this important collection of poetry and prose in 1932.

902. This "black protest" novel by Richard Wright became an immediate best-seller in 1940.

893. *Devil in a Blue Dress*

894. *African Dancer*

895. Jupiter Hammon

896. Frederick Douglass

897. *The Interesting Narrative of the Life*

898. David Walker

899. *The Big Sea*

900. *God's Trombones: Seven Negro Sermons in Verse*

901. *Cane*

902. *Native Son*

903. Who wrote *Go Tell It on the Mountain* while living in Paris?

904. What groundbreaking 1952 novel by Ralph Ellison chronicles the life of a Southern black man who cannot escape racism in the North?

905. Who is the main character of John A. Williams's 1967 novel, *The Man Who Cried I Am?*

906. Author of the 1964 Obie Award play, *The Dutchman,* he later changed his name from LeRoi Jones.

907. A colonial slave, he is the first known American black to have received formal training as an artist.

908. She journeyed to Paris on the proceeds from a bust of Colonel Robert Gould Shaw sculpted from a photograph.

909. His 1945 autobiography, *Black Boy* has become a standard text in U.S. high schools.

910. Who is the best-known black primitive painter?

911. What black primitivist, whose right arm was paralyzed by a sniper, painted images of World War I?

912. What is the name of the group of black printmakers centered at Atlanta University in the late 1930s?

903. James Baldwin

904. Invisible Man

905. Max Reddick

906. Imamu Amiri Baraka

907. Scipio Moorehead

908. Edmonia Lewis

909. Richard Wright

910. Jacob Lawrence

911. Horace Pippin

912. "Outhouse" school

913. What black abstract expressionist painted creatures that resembled bats and human beings?

914. She wrote her first poem, "A Poem by Phillis, A Negro Girl in Boston, on the Death of the Reverend George Whitefield," at the age of seventeen.

915. What black artist headed the department of art at Howard University and published *Modern Negro Art* in 1943?

916. In what state was *Les Cennelles*, the first black American anthology of poetry, compiled in 1845?

917. Having worked as an elevator operator for four dollars weekly, he achieved fame upon publication of *Lyrics of Lowly Life* in 1896.

918. This black woman, while still in her twenties, was renowned for the neoclassical sculptures she was producing in Rome in the nineteenth century.

919. Who published the poem, "The Harlem Dancer," under the pen name Eli Edwards in 1917?

920. Elizabeth Keckley, author of *Behind the Scenes; or, Thirty Years a Slave* and *Four Years in the White House*, was a designer for whom during the Civil War?

921. The first play and the first two novels to be published by an African American were written by what abolitionist?

913. Bob Thompson

914. Phillis Wheatly

915. James A. Porter

916. Louisiana

917. Paul Lawrence Dunbar

918. Edmonia Lewis

919. Claude McKay

920. Mary Todd Lincoln

921. William Wells Brown

922. Who published *Up from Slavery, a Narrative* in 1900?

923. In this 1902 novel by Paul Lawrence Dunbar, most of the characters are black.

924. This black woman wrote *Men and Mules* and *Their Eyes Were Watching God* during the Depression.

925. He authored *Nobody Knows My Name* and *The Fire Next Time*.

926. What play by ntozake shange features seven black women, each from a different city and each named after a color?

927. What is the nickname of Macon Dead III, the main character in Toni Morrison's novel, *Song of Solomon*?

928. Best known as a critic of American poetry, this black writer's own first collection of poems is titled *Lyrics of Life and Love.*

929. What landscape by Edward Bannister won a first award medal at the Centennial Exhibition in Philadelphia and sold for $1,500?

930. What collection published by Chandler Harris in 1880 made the black oral tradition available to all Americans?

931. He is a character in five of Langston Hughes's books.

922. Booker T. Washington
923. *The Sport of the Gods*
924. Zora Neale Hurston
925. James Baldwin
926. *For Colored Girls Who Have Considered the Rainbow When Suicide Wasn't Enuf*
927. Milkman
928. William Stanley Braithwaite
929. *Under the Oaks*
930. *Uncle Remus: His Songs and Sayings*
931. Jesse B. Simple

932. In 1746 at the age of sixteen, she wrote "Bars Fight," the first known piece of literature written by an African American.

933. The author of *America and Other Poems,* he felt that the colonization of Central America by blacks was their best route to freedom.

934. Frances Ellen Watkins Harper, active in the causes of abolition, women's rights, and temperance, published what volume in 1854?

935. What folk character outwitted a wolf, a bear and a fox in stories that whites did not suspect were about slaves and slavemasters?

936. What black's autobiography is thought to be Harriet Beecher Stowe's inspiration for the character of Uncle Tom?

937. On which president did William Wells Brown base his first novel, *Clotel; or, The President's Daughter?*

938. A physician, he published *The Conjure Woman* in 1932 and short stories in the *Atlantic Monthly.*

939. He wrote *The Garies and Their Friends,* the first black novel to describe ethnic prejudice against blacks in the North.

932. Lucy Terry

933. James M. Whitfield

934. *Poems on Miscellaneous Subjects*

935. Br'er Rabbit

936. Josiah Henson

937. Thomas Jefferson

938. Rudolph Fisher

939. Frank J. Webb

940. After winning a gold medal for the *Resurrection of Lazarus* at the Salon of 1894, this painter was designated chevalier of the French Legion of Honor in 1923.

941. Who termed the Northern black upper class the "talented tenth"?

942. Her only novel, *Iola Leroy, or Shadows Uplifted* (1892), was the second to be published by a black American woman.

943. In what 1912 novel does James Weldon Johnson deal with a mulatto man's indecision over whether or not to sacrifice his identity as a black for social advancement?

944. In what collection of essays does W. E. B. DuBois's famous essay, "The Sorrow Songs" appear?

945. Eric Walrond based this 1926 collection of stories on his experience among poor blacks in the West Indies.

946. His first collection of poems, *Southern Road*, was published in 1932.

947. In what country is a slave insurrection about to occur in Martin R. Delany's *Blake*, the third novel published by an African American?

948. In what satirical novel by George S. Schuyler does an electrical process convert blacks into whites who are whiter than whites, reversing racism?

940. Henry Ossawa Tanner

941. W. E. B. DuBois

942. Frances Ellen Watkins Harper

943. *The Autobiography of an Ex-Colored Man*

944. *The Souls of Black Folk*

945. *Tropic Death*

946. Sterling Brown

947. Cuba

948. *Black No More*

949. Arna Bontemps based his 1936 novel, *Black Thunder*,
      on whose attempted slave revolt in 1800?

950. Who began her studies of black folklore under Franz
      Boaz at Barnard College, and learned about voodooism
      on her own in New Orleans?

951. The painter of "Chicken Shack," he held the first one-
      man show by a black since Henry Tanner, at the New
      Gallery in New York in 1928.

952. Countee Cullen's *Color*, Claude McKay's *Harlem
      Shadows*, and W. E. B. DuBois' *The Gift of Black Folk*
      were all published in this year.

953. Known best for his four murals at the Schomburg Center
      for Black Culture in New York, he illustrated James
      Weldon Johnson's *God's Trombones* and much of Alain
      Locke's *The New Negro* in 1925.

954. In what country did the painter William H. Johnson
      choose to settle for years?

955. He won the Otto H. Kahn prize at the 1928 Harmon
      exhibit for his painting, *Swing Low, Sweet Chariot*.

956. This Harlem Renaissance artist of black, French and
      Indian descent has sculpted many important black
      figures, including Booker T. Washington and Toussaint
      L'Ouverture.

949. Gabriel Prosser   *953.* Aaron Douglas
950. Zora Neale Hurston   *954.* Norway
951. Archibald J. Motley Jr. *955.* Malvin Gray Johnson
952. 1926   *956.* Richmond Barthe

957. Recipient of the Harmon bronze award in fine arts in 1929, he sculpted *Pearl and Chester*.

958. The first black editor of Brown University's student daily, Wallace Terry, wrote this Pulitzer Prize-nominated book about black veterans.

959. This black woman was a professor of fine arts at Howard University for 45 years, and exhibited her impressionist works at the Vose Gallery in Boston in 1938.

960. How old was Alma W. Thomas when she had a one-woman show at the Whitney Museum and a retrospective at the Corcoran Gallery?

961. In what 1959 play by Lorraine Hansberry does the Younger family inherit $10,000 from an insurance policy?

962. She is the first black woman to have her film script produced in the 1972 movie, *Georgia, Georgia*.

963. What famous poet of the black experience published conversations that she had with James Baldwin in 1973 and with Margaret Walker in 1974?

964. Her first novel was *The Third Life of Grange Copeland*, published in 1970.

957. Sargent Johnson

958. *Bloods — An Oral History of the Vietnam War by Black Veterans*

959. Lois Mailou Jones

960. 81

961. *A Raisin in the Sun*

962. Maya Angelou

963. Nikki Giovanni

964. Alice Walker

965. In 1976 he was the first African American to become Poetry Consultant for the Library of Congress.

966. Who was the first black woman to win the National Book Critics Circle Award in 1977?

967. What black woman published *Gorilla, My Love*, a 1972 collection of short stories narrated by an African-American girl?

968. Elgar Enders, a rich white man who purchases a tenement house in a black ghetto, is the hero of what 1966 novel by Kristin Hunter?

969. What 1980 book by poet Audre Lorde details her struggle with cancer?

970. In 1964 he published *Catherine Carmier*, his first novel, which describes the cultural alienation of a black man returning to the South.

971. Who received the 1942 Yale Younger Poets Award for the collection, *For My People*?

972. What 1948 novel by Dorothy West deals with the Northern black bourgeoisie?

973. In what 1965 novel by William Demby does the author himself become a character writing in Rome?

974. Arna Bontemps's historical novel, *Dreams at Dusk*, is based on the Haitian slave revolt led by what man?

965. Robert Hayden

966. Toni Morrison

967. Toni Cade Bambara

968. *The Landlord*

969. *The Cancer Journals*

970. Ernest J. Gaines

971. Margaret Walker

972. *The Living Is Easy*

973. *The Catacombs*

974. Toussaint L'Ouverture

975. Who won the Iowa School of Letters Award for Short Fiction for *The Beach Umbrella*, his first book, at the age of 60?

976. *Separate But Equal*, this black artist's statement on the nineteenth-century slave trade, was the first exhibition held at New York's Cinque Gallery, in 1969.

977. What important black novelist finds the roots of all American literature in racial conflict in his essay, "Twentieth-Century Fiction and the Black Mask of Humanity"?

978. This novel by Ernest J. Gaines became a successful television film starring Cicely Tyson.

979. What 1982 novel by ntozake shange contains no punctuation?

980. In his poem, "John Brown's Body," he laments the fact that only in years to come will poets be able to write about the "black spear."

981. Margaret Walker published her first poem in this magazine.

982. Who wrote *The Long Night* (1951), *The Grand Parade* (1961), and *The Hit* (1967)?

975. Cyrus Colter

976. Malcom Bailey

977. Ralph Ellison

978. *The Autobiography of Miss Jane Pittman*

979. *Sassafras, Indigo and Cyprus*

980. Stephen Vincent Benet

981. *Crisis*

982. Julian Mayfield

983. Whose body is being buried in Ishmael Reed's 1967 novel, *The Free-Lance Pallbearers*?

984. Who wrote *Captain Blackman*, the story of a Vietnam soldier's struggle?

985. Lester Jefferson buys a wig in this 1966 novel by Charles Wright because the salesman has told him that it will allow him to fit into society.

986. What black poet published *Dancing* and *The Song Turning Back into Itself*?

987. Which of James Baldwin's first two novels deals with homosexual love?

988. Who is the main character of Gwendolyn Brooks's only novel?

989. He won the Grand Prize for Poetry at the First World African Festival of Arts for his 1965 collection, *A Ballad of Remembrance*.

990. Margaret Walker presented this 1966 novel for her Ph.D. dissertation at the University of Iowa.

991. She traveled throughout the West Indies and rediscovered the culture of her ancestors before publishing *Brown Girl, Brownstones* in 1959.

983. Bukka Dopeyduke's

984. John A. Williams

985. *The Wig*

986. Al Young

987. *Giovanni's Room*

988. Maud Martha

989. Robert Hayden

990. *Jubilee*

991. Paule Marshall

992. What black playwright married publisher Robert Nemiroff in 1953?

993. What black satirist studied under Archibald MacLeish and John Hawkes, and published *A Different Drummer* in 1962?

994. Her sculpture, *The Wretched*, exhibited at the Paris Salon of 1903, won praise from Auguste Rodin.

995. A sculptress concerned with the position of the mulatto, she is also known for her portrait busts of Paul Lawrence Dunbar, W. E. B. DuBois, and Francis Grimke.

996. This white artist painted *The Gulf Stream*, a work of major importance in the breakdown of stereotyped portrayals of blacks in art.

997. What African-American artist and teacher sculpted *African Savage* and *Tom Tom*?

998. Eldzier Cortor, a graduate of the Art Institute of Chicago and painter of *Slum Song* (1962), was an easel painter for this organization in 1937.

999. The Rev. G. W. Hobbs's 1785 pastel of this political leader is considered to be the first portrait of a black by another black.

992. Lorraine Hansberry

993. William Melvin Kelley

994. Meta Warrick Fuller

995. May Howard Jackson

996. Winslow Homer

997. Augusta Savage

998. Works Progress Administration

999. Richard Allen

1000. Who was the first African American to be recognized as a portrait painter?

1001. His is the only known self-portrait by a colonial black.

1002. Who is the author of *The New York Times* best-seller of 1992, *Waiting to Exhale*?

1003. Robert M. Douglass Jr. sold his lithographs of this man in 1833 at fifty cents a copy for the abolitionist cause.

1004. Whose engraving captioned, "Am I not a man and a brother?" became the emblem of the antislavery movement in Britain?

1005. A cousin of Frederick Douglass, he is thought to have executed a portrait of Abraham Lincoln, commissioned by the president himself.

1006. William Simpson, the black abolitionist who executed the Loguen portraits in 1835, was first recognized by what black writer?

1007. Robert Stuart Duncanson's 1853 painting, *Uncle Tom and Little Eva*, is an illustration for what book?

1008. He painted *Grand Canyon of the Yellow-Stone* from Hayden Point in 1891.

1000. Joshua Johnston

1001. Julien Hudson

1002. Terry McMillan

1003. William Lloyd Garrison

1004. Patrick Henry Reason's

1005. David Bustill Bowser

1006. William Wells Brown

1007. *Uncle Tom's Cabin*

1008. Grafton Tyler Brown

1009. What sculpture by Meta Warrick Fuller portrays a woman freeing herself from mummy-like bands of cloth?

1010. Although he won critical acclaim in Boston for his portrait of *Lizzie May Ulmer* in 1776, he had difficulty obtaining commissions.

1011. In 1939 who sculpted two eight-foot figures seated on llamas?

1012. What is Edmonia Lewis's Chippewa name?

1013. Although he died at 37, this black painter was aware of modern artistic trends, particularly of the Barbizon School in France, and received much critical acclaim.

1014. Having studied from 1924 to 1925 at l'Academie de la Grande Chaumiere in Paris, portraits she painted such as *Frankie* (1937) took on a Romantic aspect.

1015. Having developed an interest in black subject matter while studying in France, Palmer Hayden painted a series of twelve scenes from the life of this black folk hero between 1944 and 1954.

1016. The son of a black artist, he was fascinated with Haiti, and exhibits expressionist and realist tendencies in paintings such as *Bird Vendor*.

1009. Awakening of Ethiopia

1010. Nelson A. Primus

1011. Sargent Johnson

1012. Wildfire

1013. William A. Harper

1014. Laura Wheeler Waring

1015. John Henry

1016. Ellis Wilson

1017. Famous for his 1933 piece in lacquered cloth over wood, *Forever Free*, he married the sculptress May Howard Jackson.

1018. Citizens of San Francisco's Chinatown helped this painter out of his financial difficulties, and he painted *Oriental Child* there in 1900.

1019. What African-American artist whose woodcuts include *African Fantasy* (1929) was also an innovative teacher of art?

1020. What group founded in 1963 by Romare Bearden and Norman Lewis asserted that it would paint only in black and white, in order to address racial conflict?

1021. At what university was the first major black art gallery established?

1022. This sculptor received much media attention but preferred not to discuss his aims with interviewers, instead letting works such as *Supplication* speak for themselves.

1023. Trained at Columbia University as well as in Paris and Vienna, her 1972 alabaster sculpture, *Peace,* is among her best works.

1017. Sargent Claude Johnson
1018. Nelson A. Primus
1019. James Lesesne Wells
1020. Spiral Group

1021. Howard University
1022. William E. Artis
1023. Selma Burke

1024. Until he won a solo exhibition at the Museum of Modern Art in 1938, William Edmonson supported himself by painting these.

1025. His 1949 mural for the black role in the settlement of California, *Exploration and Colonization*, is adjacent to Hale Woodruff's *Settlement and Development* in Los Angeles.

1026. What 1937 mural by Charles Alston is in the Harlem Hospital?

1027. He studied with Augusta Savage, and painted such diverse works as *Yellow Hat* (1940) and *Processional* (1965).

1028. His experimentation with photography in collages is represented by *The Prevalence of Ritual: Tidings* (1967).

1029. Who said of his 1940–41 series, *The Migration of the Negro,* "The black man in America is always trying to better his condition and the conditions of his children"?

1030. What 1943 mural by Charles White features Crispus Attucks, Denmark Vesey, Booker T. Washington, and George Washington Carver among others?

1031. Active in the civil rights movement, she counts among her works the cedar sculpture, *Black Unity* (1968) and the lithograph, *Negro es Bello* (1968).

1032. *Roz* (1972) and *Trabajadores* (1973) are representative of the social expression in this black painter and printmaker's work.

1033. After visiting Africa in 1970, he produced a series on the country in red pencil, one of which, *Page from an African Notebook*, integrates human profiles and figures into the patterns of African fabric.

1034. Paintings such as *Natural Woman* (1972), with its strong captivating color and the mixing of black profiles into abstract patterning, reflect the influence of Africa on this African-American artist's work.

1035. His ink, paint, and graphite work, *One Common Thought* (1972), refers to the circular eye, a symbolic element in African sculpture.

1036. Paul Keene's 1969 painting, *Garden of Shango,* represents which ancient Yoruba deity?

1037. The black madonna and child in this black artist's 1971 acrylic painting, *Guardian?,* are protected by an ankh, a black liberation flag, the African continent, and a jackal.

1031. Elizabeth Catlett

1032. John Wilson

1033. Raymond Saunders

1034. Lucille Malika Roberts

1035. Floyd Coleman

1036. God of thunder

1037. Mikelle Fletcher

1038. In reference to the subjects of her 1974 painting, *Gossip in the Sanctuary,* she says, "In church, they felt free to dream, to hope, and to show all the human instincts . . ."

1039. Reginald Gammon's 1970 painting, *Scottsboro Mothers,* depicts the mothers of a real-life group of black men who were charged with what crime?

1040. What black feminist created the mixed-media *Family of Women* series in the 1970s?

1041. Where is the African-American mural, *Wall of Respect?*

1042. This black sculptress, who dedicated her first one-woman show to Malcolm X, has lived in Paris since 1961.

1043. Hughie Lee-Smith and Charles Sallee are both graduates of what black art school in Cleveland?

1044. What twentieth century creator from St. Thomas tried to fuse poetry, music, and art in his paintings for the *Blues for Nat Turner Jazz Suite?*

1045. In his 1778 painting, *Watson and the Shark,* this white artist placed a black figure in a heroic position beside whites.

1038. Varnette Honeywood
1039. Rape
1040. Faith Ringgold
1041. Chicago
1042. Barbara Chase-Riboud
1043. Karamu House
1044. Adelmola Olugebefola
1045. John Singleton Copley

1046. What white artist painted *Both Members of the Club* (1909), the subject of which is a black boxer and a white boxer "trying to beat each other's brains out for money"?

1047. He organized the first large-scale exhibition of African-American art in New York City in 1862.

1048. What black poet was elected mayor of Langston, Oklahoma, four times?

1049. Henry Gudgel, son of a white man and a black slave, carved what object reminiscent of African art for Union soldier John Bryan in 1863?

1050. His *Early Afternoon at Montigny* won a thirty-dollar prize for "most worthy landscape shown" at the Art Institute of Chicago's 1905 exhibition.

1051. Aaron Douglas helped collect African-American art to illustrate what notable Harlem Renaissance publication?

1052. Who organized the 1941 exhibition, "Afro-American Art on Both Continents," which included the works of Romare Bearden and the Delaney brothers?

1053. In what year did Eldzier Cortor, Lois Mailou Jones, Jacob Lawrence, and Hughie Lee-Smith all participated in the Chicago exhibition "Art of the American Negro"?

1046. George Bellows   *1050.* William A. Harper
1047. Edward M. Thomas   *1051. The New Negro*
1048. Melvin B. Tolson   *1052.* Alain Locke
1049. Walking stick   *1053.* 1940

1054. How many black artists had one-man shows between 1918 and 1954?

1055. After meeting black artists like Archibald Motley, Gwendolyn Brooks and Richard Wright in the Chicago studio of dancer Katherine Dunham, he helped George Neal form the Arts and Crafts Guild.

1056. She produced *Figures such as Mrs. Jackson* (1968), a carved and painted slab of plywood wearing real clothes.

1057. Where is the National Center of Afro-American Art?

1058. In what year were the Museum of African Art and the Frederick Douglass Institute in Washington, D.C., founded?

1059. What important exhibition was held at the Studio Museum to protest the Whitney Museum's exclusion of black artists from its show of works from the Great Depression?

1060. Tom Lloyd founded this innovative museum of black history and culture in Jamaica, New York.

1061. Norman Lewis, Romare Bearden, and Ernest Crichlow founded what showroom for young minority artists in Manhattan's East Village?

1054. Six

1055. Charles White

1056. Marie Johnson

1057. Boston

1058. 1964

1059. "Invisible Americans: Black Artists of the '30s"

1060. Store-Front Museum

1061. Cinque Gallery

1062. What Philadelphia museum was named after the African "City of the Gods?"

1063. This Chicago community organization was set up to help blacks learn through art.

1064. Topper Carew founded this Washington, D.C., center for art education and alternative high school for blacks.

1065. Considered the most important black art exhibit of the mid-sixties, this New York show was organized by Romare Bearden and Carroll Greene Jr.

1066. In what city did Dana Chandler and Gary Rickson paint their Black Power mural next to a playground?

1067. Where is the *Wall of Dignity*?

1068. Charles White, who said, "Paint is the only weapon I have in which to fight what I resent," was influenced by the muralists of what country?

1069. The murals *Black Music* and *Black Leaders* hang in a cafeteria of what college?

1070. What 1970 painting by Dana Chandler is dedicated to a slain Black Panther leader?

1071. What black artist produced works like *Pray for America* (1969) by covering himself with margarine?

1062. The Ile-Ife Museum of Afro-American Art and Culture

1063. Art and Soul

1064. The New Thing Art and Architecture Center

1065. "The Evolution of the Afro-American Artist: 1800–1950"

1066. Boston

1067. Detroit

1068. Mexico

1069. Knoxville College

1070. Fred Hampton's Door

1071. David Hammons

1072. Black Emergency Cultural Coalition leaders Joseph and Benny Andrews wrote to Governor Nelson Rockefeller in 1971 to request funding for an art program at what institution?

1073. In her 1976 memoir, *Generations*, she tells of how her great-grandmother was hanged for having murdered her white lover.

1074. In what year was the Judson Three convicted of desecrating the American flag on their canvases?

1075. This artist of African and American Indian descent, who has painted such abstract landscapes as *The Gorge* (1966), is also a jazz singer.

1076. The engraver of *David in the Wilderness* (1955–56), her works are included in the permanent collections of museums in Washington, New York, Scotland, and England.

1077. A black sculptor who combines art with technology, he was the first artist-in-residence at the Studio Museum in Harlem.

1078. His works, among them *A Fine and Secret Place* (1967) and *Little Boys Are Very Impressionable* (1967), attach evocative words to abstract images.

1072. Attica Prison

1073. Lucille Clifton

1074. 1970

1075. Richard Mayhew

1076. Norma Morgan

1077. Tom Lloyd

1078. Marvin Harden

1079. How old was Richard Hunt when he sold his sculpture, *Arachne*, to the Museum of Modern Art in 1956?

1080. What is the geometric shape of Betty Blayton's large-scale 1970 oil collages *Concentrated Energies* and *Iconograph*?

1081. What 1965 collage by Alvin Hollingsworth is a black variation on one of Picasso's works?

1082. On what 1965 events did black painter Merton B. Simpson base his *Confrontation* series?

1083. Painter Benny Andrews designed album covers for this record company.

1084. This black artist printed a pamphlet called *Black is a Color*.

1085. What black artist has produced life-sized body parts with African designs on them, such as *Black Leg* (1969)?

1086. Who was the first president of the Boston Negro Artist Association and cultural chairman of the Malcolm X Foundation?

1087. What rusty metal object did Lovett Thompson push through the neck of his 1970 wood carving, *The Junkie*?

1088. In what public institutions did poet Etheridge Knight receive eight years of schooling?

1079. 20

1080. A circle

1081. *Why: Black Guernica*

1082. Harlem riots

1083. Blue Note

1084. Raymond Saunders

1085. Ben Jones

1086. Gary A. Rickson

1087. A nail

1088. Penitentiaries

1089. At what young age was Amiri Baraka (LeRoi Jones) when he graduated from Howard University?

1090. What painting by Henry Ossawa Tanner hangs in the Luxembourg Museum in Paris?

1091. What is the subject of Meta Vaux Warrick Fuller's first clay work?

1092. In 1903–4 Pauline Hopkins was editor of this Boston magazine showcasing black talent.

1093. In 1924 he wrote *By Sanction of Law*, a melodramatic novel about members of the black bourgeoisie.

1094. Both Bryant Rollins's 1967 *Danger Song* and Dorothy West's 1948 *The Living Is Easy* are situated in what neighborhood?

1095. Black poets Angelina Grimke and Anne Spencer were both published for the first time in this anthology edited by Countee Cullen.

1096. How many black authors did Chester Eisinger include in his 1963 anthology, *Fiction of the Forties*?

1097. The aim of this art school founded by Russell and Rowena Jeliffe in Cleveland in 1915 was to put blacks on an equal creative footing with whites, and to allow them to convey their unique experiences through art.

*

1089. 17

1090. The Raising of Lazarus

1091. Medussa's head

1092. The Colored American

1093. J. McHenry Jones

1094. Boston's South End

1095. Caroling Dusk

1096. Three

1097. Karamu House

1098. Having won the encouragement of Richard Wright while studying at the Sorbonne, he published his first volume of poetry under the pen name Paul Vesey in Germany in 1956.

1099. During what decade did the black militant Broadside Poets write?

1100. In her poem, "Black Jam for Dr. Negro," she attacks the black middle class.

1101. The title of black poet Conrad Kent Rivers's poem, "By African Moonlight on Forgotten Shores," refers to the death of what black figure?

1102. What black librarian, writer, and translator of Russian and French started Broadside Press in 1965?

1103. Before he was thirty, Haki Madhubuti had published four volumes of poetry under this original name.

1104. A contributor to Frederick Douglass's *North Star* and author of *Autobiography of A Fugitive Slave* (1855), he moved from New York to Canada in 1851 to escape the fugitive slave laws.

1105. He anticipated the Harlem Renaissance in poetic collections like *Visions of the Dusk* (1915) and *Songs of the Soil* (1916).

1098. Samuel Allen   *1102.* Dudley Randall
1099. The 1960s   *1103.* Don L. Lee
1100. Mari E. Evans   *1104.* Samuel Ward
1101. W. E. B. Du Bois   *1105.* Fenton Johnson

1106. Writer Jean Toomer was born into the mulatto elite in what city?

1107. Who published *Stranger and Alone* in 1950?

1108. In this 1964 novel, his first, John O. Killens traces a black family in Georgia through two generations.

1109. Once an assistant editor of *Poetry* magazine, she coauthored *Poem: Counterpoem* with Dudley Randall.

1110. What volume of poetry did Mari Evans publish in 1970?

1111. Whose autobiography, *Report from Part One,* was published in 1972?

1112. This 1972 book by Albert Murray describes a black man's encounters with blacks and whites on a journey from Harlem to Alabama.

1113. He is recognized for his critical works, the most important of which is *The Way of the New World: The Black Novel in America* (1975).

1114. What anthology of the Black Arts Movement did Amiri Baraka and Larry Neal coedit in 1968?

1115. What poet published *The Black Unicorn* in 1978?

1106. Washington, D.C.

1107. Saunders Redding

1108. *Youngblood*

1109. Margaret Danner

1110. *I Am a Black Woman*

1111. Gwendolyn Brooks

1112. *South to a Very Old Place*

1113. Addison Gayle

1114. *Black Fire*

1115. Audre Lorde

1116. In addition to authoring several books for young people and working with poetry and film, she published a biography of Fannie Lou Hamer in 1972.

1117. What African American from Detroit founded the Yoruba Temple in Harlem in 1960 and helped stimulate the utilization of Yoruba tradition among New York artists?

1118. What black novelist of the bourgeois tradition was literary editor for the NAACP's *Crisis* magazine under W. E. B. DuBois?

1119. Who published *Sarah Phillips,* the story of an upper-middle-class adolescent whose struggles to separate herself from her black race are ultimately successful?

1120. This 1969 children's book by Kristin Hunter deals with Louretta Hawkins's quest for self while growing up in the ghetto.

1121. David Bradley won a PEN/Faulkner award in 1982 for this novel.

1122. Who is the subject of black sculptor John Wilson's 1985 bust, which was the first portrait of a black man to be installed in the Capitol in Washington, D.C.?

1116. June Jordan
1117. Adefunimi
1118. Jessie Fauset
1119. Andrea Lee

1120. The Soul Brothers and Sister Lou
1121. The Chaneysville Incident
1122. Martin Luther King Jr.

1123. What drama about the murder of a psychotic black Army sergeant won Charles H. Fuller Jr. the Pulitzer Prize in 1982, and has since become a major motion picture?

1124. This important black sculptor is thought to have derived some of his ideas from a six-year stint working in the University of Chicago's zoological experimental laboratory.

1125. While serving time in the Ohio State Penitentiary between 1928 and 1936 for armed robbery, he published short stories in *Esquire, Coronet, Abbott's Monthly Magazine,* and *The Bronzeman.*

1126. Melvin B. Tolson, author of *Harlem Gallery* (1965), was poet laureate of this African nation which had originally served as a refuge for ex-slaves and free blacks.

1127. Black poets Dudley Randall and Margaret Danner both worked at this Detroit cultural center in the early 1960s.

1128. In this, John Wideman's third novel, Philadelphia blacks plot the lynching of a white policeman.

1129. Alice Childress was made Honorary Citizen of Atlanta when this, her play about interracial love, opened there in 1975.

1123. A Soldier's Play
1124. Richard Hunt
1125. Chester Himes
1126. Liberia

1127. Boone House
1128. The Lynchers
1129. Wedding Band: A Love/Hate Story in Black and White

1130. He won an Obie for *The Fabulous Miss Marie* in 1975.

1131. In 1965 he was recruited by Harvard Law School and his second short story, "Gold Coast," was awarded first prize by *The Atlantic Monthly*.

1132. Author of the 1974 collection of poems, *An Ordinary Woman*, she has also written sixteen books for children.

1133. Poet Victor Hernandez Cruz edited this 1960s periodical published by a black artist's collective on New York's Lower East Side.

1134. In 1970 his sixth volume of poetry, *Words in the Mourning Time*, was nominated for the National Book Award.

1135. In her *Journal*, Charlotte Forten Grimke, later the wife of the Rev. Francis Grimke, narrates her two successful years educating ex-slaves in what region captured by the Union army?

1136. In 1890 she wrote *Clarence and Corinne, or God's Way*, the first Sunday school book published by an African American.

1137. He is considered to be the first African American to have written poetry in black plantation dialect.

1130. Ed Bullins

1131. James Allen McPherson

1132. Lucille Clifton

1133. *Umbra*

1134. Robert Hayden

1135. South Sea Islands

1136. Amelia E. Johnson

1137. James Edwin Campbell

1138. A dramatist and short story writer as well, he published three volumes of poetry: *A Little Dreaming (1913)*, *Visions of Dusk (1915)*, and *Songs of the Soil (1916)*.

1139. After 1922, this black journalist and fiction writer from Georgetown, British Guyana, published in numerous periodicals, among them *The New Republic, Opportunity, Vanity Fair, The Saturday Review of Literature, Argosy All-Story Magazine,* and *Current History.*

1140. What black periodical of the arts, which lasted only one issue in the twenties, contained the works of Zora Neale Hurston, Aaron Douglas, John P. Davis, Gwendolyn Bennett, Bruce Nugent, and Langston Hughes?

1141. Besides being a movie director, composer, author and semi-pro basketball player, he was a photographer for *Life* magazine from 1948 to 1972.

1142. "Three Fightingmen," a bronze statue of two white soldiers and one black, was installed at what U.S. memorial in 1984?

1143. What African-American novelist won the Pulitzer Prize and the American Book Award in 1983?

1144. Paule Marshall won the 1984 American Book Award for this novel.

1138. Fenton Johnson

1139. Eric Walrond

1140. Fire

1141. Gordon Parks

1142. The Vietnam Veterans' Memorial in Washington, D.C.

1143. Alice Walker

1144. Praisesong for the Widow

1145. She won the 1983 American Book Award for First Fiction for her novel, *The Women of Brewster Place.*

1146. Her novel, *The Street,* was published in 1946.

1147. Best known for his 1969 novel, *The Life and Loves of Mr. Jiveass Nigger,* he attacks the racial stereotyping of blacks by white authors and filmmakers in his writing.

1148. What magazine named Hal Bennett most promising writer of 1970 for his short story, "Dotson Gerber Resurrected"?

1149. He started out as a gesture writer for the *Newark Herald News* at sixteen, published *A Wilderness of Vines,* his first novel, in 1966, and won the Faulkner Award in 1973.

1150. Internationally acclaimed sculptress Barbara Chase-Riboud based what 1979 historical novel on Thomas Jefferson's life?

1151. Which of Ronald L. Fair's novels won a Best Book Award from the American Library Association in 1972?

1152. Author of *There Is a Tree More Ancient than Eden* (1973), he combines religious and secular symbols in images such as a switchblade used to serve the bread of the Eucharist.

1145. Gloria Naylor

1146. Ann Petry

1147. Cecil Brown

1148. Playboy

1149. Hal Bennett

1150. Sally Hemings

1151. We Can't Breathe

1152. Leon Forrest

1153. This 1970 novel by Louise Meriwether tells the story of a twelve-year-old girl in Harlem during the Depression.

1154. Author of *Hurry Home*, he was the second African American to win a Rhodes Scholarship, in 1963.

1155. Which of Alice Childress's plays won the first Obie Award in 1956 for best original off-Broadway play?

1156. This play by Ed Bullins, part of *The Electronic Nigger and Others*, won the Rice Drama Desk Award in 1968.

1157. Her *Killing Floor,* was the 1978 Lamont Poetry Selection of the Academy of American Poets.

1158. What black journalist, born in the Civil War, had his poetry collected and published in *Echoes from the Cabin and Elsewhere* in 1905?

1153. Daddy Was a Number Runner
1154. John Edgar Wideman
1155. Trouble in Mind
1156. Clara's Ole Man
1157. Ai (Florence Anthony)
1158. James Edwin Campbell

Sports

1159. He was the first black player in modern major-league baseball.

1160. De Hart Hubbard was the first black athlete to win this Olympic track and field event in Paris in 1924.

1161. Levi Jackson became the first black football captain at this Ivy League college.

1162. He was the first black head coach at the University of Maryland.

1163. Former Boston Celtic Sam Jones was the first black voted into this state's hall of fame.

1164. He was the first black college basketball official.

1165. Who was the first woman to win both the 200 and 400 meter races, setting Olympic and U.S. records in both events?

1166. Who was the first black tennis player on the Virginia Slims Tour?

1159. Jackie Robinson
1160. Broad jump
1161. Yale University
1162. Bill Jones
1163. North Carolina
1164. William "Dolly" King
1165. Valerie Briscoe-Hooks
1166. Bonnie Logan

1167. This heavyweight champ was nicknamed the "Brown Bomber."

1168. Who was the first black player to pitch a perfect game?

1169. Name the Negro League player, nicknamed "Giant Killer," who pitched a perfect, no-hit game.

1170. Roosevelt "Rosey" Brown was the first black captain of this National Football League team.

1171. Who was major league baseball's first black catcher?

1172. Boxer Arnold R. Cream adopted this ring name.

1173. In 1982 who became the first pro quarterback to throw for 5,000 yards in a single season?

1174. Who was the first black umpire in major league baseball?

1175. He was the first black U.S. Men's Amateur Tennis champion.

1176. This athlete was the first black U.S. Olympic basketball team member to break into the Amateur Basketball League as well as star on an AAU championship team.

1177. On December 26, 1908, this boxer defeated Tommy Burns to become the first black heavyweight champion.

1167. Joe Louis
1168. Dan McClellan
1169. Webster McDonald
1170. New York Giants
1171. Roy Campanella
1172. "Jersey Joe Walcott"

1173. Warren Moon
1174. Emmett Ashford
1175. Arthur Ashe
1176. Don Barksdale
1177. Jack Johnson

1178. She was the first black woman to win the American Tennis Association (ATA) singles title.

1179. Who was the first black U.S. heavyweight boxing champion?

1180. He was the first black sprinter to break into the "world's fastest human" category by coholding the world's record in the 100-yard dash (9.6 secs.) in 1914.

1181. Who was the first person to broad jump over 25 feet?

1182. He was the first black sprinter to win an Olympic gold medal in the 100-meter dash in 1932.

1183. In 1904 he became the first black track and field entrant in the modern Olympic.

1184. What college did Biddle University play in the first black college football game?

1185. In what year was the first black professional baseball team organized?

1186. The waiters of the Babylon, New York, hotel formed this first black professional baseball team.

1187. What was the name of the first black professional baseball team?

1178. Ora Washington

1179. George Godfrey

1180. Howard P. Drew

1181. Edward Gourdin

1182. Eddie Tolan

1183. Harold Paige

1184. Livingstone College

1185. 1895

1186. Argyle Hotel

1187. The Cuban Giants

1188. What university appointed the first black varsity captain in the Big Ten?

1189. Who won the first black intercollegiate golf championship?

1190. Who, in 1964, was the first black tennis player to be name to the American Davis Cup squad?

1191. Jesse Owens was the first athlete to surpass this landmark distance in the broad jump.

1192. The first black intercollegiate varsity rower attended this university.

1193. How many points did Michael Jordan score against the N.Y. Knicks nine days after his return to professional basketball in 1995?

1194. This black female athlete was a member of six all-collegiate teams during her years at Temple University.

1195. He rode six horses to victory in a single day of racing at Washington Park, Chicago, on July 10, 1891.

1196. Who was the first African-American captain of a collegiate track and field team?

1197. He was nominated as the first black captain of a varsity football squad while playing for Amherst College in 1891.

1188. University of Chicago	*1193.* 55
1189. Alfred Holmes	*1194.* Inez Patterson
1190. Arthur Ashe	*1195.* "Monk" Overton
1191. 26 feet	*1196.* Clifton Wharton
1192. Syracuse University	*1197.* William H. Lewis

1198. Who was the first black to captain a collegiate basketball team?

1199. What university in 1908 became the first school to have a black basketball team captain?

1200. What university's team elected the first black collegiate track and field captain in the United States?

1201. This association was the first organized to promote and control athletes at black schools.

1202. While playing for the Brooklyn Dodgers, he became the first African-American pitcher to win a World Series game.

1203. Who was the first black athlete to represent the United States in Olympic gymnastics?

1204. Who was the first black athlete to win the Heisman Trophy?

1205. Who was the third black to break major-league baseball's "color line?"

1206. "Sweetwater" Clifton played for what famous basketball squad after retiring from the NBA?

1207. Wilt Chamberlain left college to play with this professional basketball team.

1198. Fenwick H. Watkins

1199. University of Vermont

1200. Boston University

1201. The Interscholastic Athletic Association of Mid-Atlantic States

1202. Joe Black

1203. Michael Eric Carter

1204. Ernie Davis

1205. Willard Jesse Brown

1206. The Harlem Globetrotters

1207. The Harlem Globetrotters

1208. After the 1996 Summer Olympics, who is the world's greatest athlete, decathlon gold medalist?

1209. Joe Gilliam Jr. was the NFL's first African American to play this position.

1210. He was Spain's first U.S.-born black matador.

1211. Richard Ewell and Michelle McCladdie became the first African-American couple in this professional sports organization.

1212. Theodore Flowers was the first black boxer to win the championship in which weight class?

1213. He was the first Bahamian pitcher in the American League.

1214. At what major university was Dennis Franklin the first black quarterback?

1215. What was heavyweight champ Joe Frazier's nickname?

1216. Robert "Pappy" Gault was the first U.S. Olympic coach of what team?

1217. What Cuban-born boxer, nicknamed "The Hawk," created the "Bolo Punch?"

1218. What tennis champion and golfer earned her place in the Black Hall of Fame in 1974?

1208. Dan O'Brien

1209. Quarterback

1210. Richard Evans

1211. The Ice Capades

1212. Middleweight

1213. Wenty Ford

1214. University of Michigan

1215. "Smokin' Joe"

1216. Boxing

1217. Kid Gavilan

1218. Althea Gibson

1219. Who was the first black to play with the Washington Senators?

1220. Who was the Los Angeles Dodger's first black coach?

1221. What was the nickname of the first black NFL quarterback?

1222. At what university was Walt Fordon the first black player and coach?

1223. This first black justice in Massachusetts was the first athlete to broad jump over 25 feet.

1224. Who was the fourth African American to enter organized baseball?

1225. Name the record-breaking 1960s jockey from Atlantic City, New Jersey.

1226. Who coached Morehouse's first football team?

1227. Which former Harlem Globetrotter was touted as "The World's Best Dribbler," and founded the Harlem Magicians?

1228. Who was the first black professional basketball coach in the now defunct American Basketball League?

1229. Who was the first African-American player traded in major-league baseball?

1219. Joe Black

1220. James "Junior" Gilliam

1221. "Jefferson Street Joe"

1222. University of California

1223. Edward O. Gourdin

1224. Frank Grant

1225. Robert McCurdy

1226. Benwell Townes Harvey

1227. Marques Haynes

1228. John B. McLendon

1229. Orestes "Minnie" Minoso

1230. He was the first black member of the NAIA (National Association of Intercollegiate Athletics) Executive Committee.

1231. Who was the first black contestant in a billiards tournament?

1232. In 1956 at age 21, who became the youngest fighter to win the world heavyweight title?

1233. What Brown University football player was the first black to participate in the Rose Bowl?

1234. He was the first black major-league baseball manager.

1235. Who was the first African-American coach in a professional sports league?

1236. In 1966 it became the first professional athletic team to appoint a black coach.

1237. As the first U.S. black boxer to receive recognition, he is referred to in the *Life and Journals of Lord Byron.*

1238. Frank Grant first invented this indispensable piece of baseball equipment.

1239. After the first black baseball team was organized in 1885, what name was attached to nearly every all-black team for 25 years?

1230. Arnett William Mumford

1231. Cicero "Brooklyn Kid" Murphy

1232. Floyd Patterson

1233. Frederick "Fritz" Pollard

1234. Frank Robinson

1235. Bill Russell

1236. Boston Celtics

1237. Bill Richmond

1238. Shinguards

1239. "Giants"

1240. In 1879 this black jockey won 35 of the 75 races he entered, including the Travers Stakes at Saratoga.

1241. The first significant black-white boxing match ended in a draw in which round?

1242. In 1925 the Boston Athletic Club refused admission to a football player from this university on the grounds that he was black.

1243. In what year were the Harlem Globetrotters organized?

1244. The first black Heisman Trophy winner was afflicted with this disease.

1245. This pitcher led his team to a Negro League World Series for the second time in 1947 after pitching 64 consecutive scoreless innings during the season.

1246. Who was the welterweight boxing champion from 1946 through 1951?

1247. How long did Joe Louis retain the world heavyweight boxing championship before he retired in 1949?

1248. What team signed the first African-American player in the National Basketball Association?

1249. Who was the first black to be accepted to compete in the National Tennis Championship at Forest Hills, New York?

1240. Isaac Murphy

1241. 61st

1242. Boston College

1243. 1927

1244. Leukemia

1245. Satchel Paige

1246. Sugar Ray Robinson

1247. 11 years, 8 months

1248. Boston Celtics

1249. Althea Gibson

1250. Who was the U.S. light heavyweight boxing champion from 1952 to 1961?

1251. Who was the first black member of the Professional Golfers Association?

1252. From 1956 to his retirement in 1966, this All-League fullback broke every rushing record in the NFL.

1253. He was NBA scoring champion for seven years in a row, from 1959 to 1965.

1254. In 1968, he became the No. 1 American tennis player after winning the National Open and the Men's Singles championship at Forest Hills, New York.

1255. Bernie Bickerstaff has been both coach and general manager of this NBA team.

1256. In 1969 this major golf tournament became the first won by an African American.

1257. A two-time Kentucky Derby winner, he was the first American to win the English Sweepstakes.

1258. Who was the World Tennis Team's first black player?

1259. Chicago's first black judge, Fred Wayman "Duke" Slate, played pro football for this team.

1260. She was the first black woman to hold a first-degree black belt in judo.

1261. Who was the first black female member of the Amateur Fencers League?

1262. Who was the only baseball player to play in all four Negro World Series?

1263. He was the first black trainer for harness racing horses.

1264. Cincinnati Reds outfielder Bobby Tolan was the first black recipient of this award.

1265. Who was the first black National Football League head coach?

1266. He was the first black professional major-league hockey player.

1267. Who was the first black female jockey, winning for the first time on September 2, 1971?

1268. This fencer was the youngest winner of the National Women's Foil Championship.

1269. Track star Malvin Greston Whitfield was the first black winner of this award.

1270. He was the first black umpire in the National League.

1260. Victoria Young Smith

1261. Sophonia Pierce Stent

1262. George "Never" Sweatt

1263. Marion "Dover Tolson

1264. The Hutch Award

1265. Emlen Tunnell

1266. Alton White

1267. Cheryl White

1268. Ruth White

1269. The Sullivan Award

1270. Art Williams

1271. Who was the first African American to win the National Public Links Golf Tournament?

1272. NFL player Paul "Tank" Younger was the first black inducted into this state's Hall of Fame.

1273. In 1965 this Chicago Bears rookie scored six touchdowns in one game and 22 for the season.

1274. Who was the first African-American official in the National Football League?

1275. When was the first black-sponsored float entered in the annual Pasadena, California, Rose Bowl Parade?

1276. For what team did Oscar Robertson play in 1964 when he was the only player unanimously voted to the NBA's All-Star Team?

1277. Who was the first African-American golfer to reach $1 million in career earnings?

1278. Who holds the record of 100 points scored in a single NBA game?

1279. In what stadium did the Harlem Globetrotters play for the largest ever basketball audience of 75,000 fans?

1280. He became the first black athlete to win an intercollegiate weight championship when he threw the hammer 162 feet, four and one-half inches in 1912.

1271. Bill Wright	1276. Cincinnati Royals
1272. Louisiana	1277. Lee Elders
1273. Gale Sayers	1278. Wilt Chamberlain
1274. Burl Toler	1279. Berlin Olympic Stadium
1275. 1964	1280. Theodore Cable

1281. Who was the first African American to play at Wimbledon?

1282. Joe DiMaggio called him "the best pitcher I ever faced."

1283. When was the first world series between Negro League team played?

1284. Hank Aaron began his baseball career with this black team.

1285. In 1977 he broke Ty Cobb's career record of 892 stolen bases.

1286. At quarterback, Warren Moon led this Canadian Football League team to five straight championships.

1287. Who was the NFL's first black regular starting quarterback?

1288. In 1982 he signed a $13.2 million, 6-year contract with the Philadelphia 76ers to become sport's highest-paid team athlete for a single season.

1289. He became the Professional Rodeo Cowboys Association's first black champion in 1983.

1290. Who is the only pitcher credited with two World Series home runs?

1291. The first black Chicago Cub, he was the first slugger to use a light bat.

1281. Althea Gibson
1282. Satchel Paige
1283. 1924
1284. Mobile Bears
1285. Lou Brock
1286. Edmonton Eskimos
1287. James Harris
1288. Moses Malone
1289. Charles Sampson
1290. Bob Gibson
1291. Ernie Banks

1292. She was the country's first black woman sports car racer.

1293. Who was the first black player in the American Baseball League?

1294. She was the first African-American professional ice skater.

1295. A catcher, he was the first black to play for the New York Yankees baseball team.

1296. This African-American jockey won the very first Kentucky Derby.

1297. Who was major-league baseball's first black coach?

1298. Who was the first African-American major-league hockey star?

1299. For what baseball team did the first black in the American League play?

1300. Who is the only jockey to have ridden three winners in the Kentucky Derby?

1301. Who ended Joe Louis's career by knocking him out in Madison Square Garden in 1951?

1302. In what year did the first African Americans become members of the National Basketball Association?

1292. La Ruth Bostic

1293. Larry Doby

1294. Mabel Fairbanks

1295. Elston Howard

1296. Isaac Murphy

1297. John "Buck" O'Neill

1298. Willie O'Ree

1299. Cleveland Indians

1300. Isaac Murphy

1301. Rocky Marciano

1302. 1950

1303. Who was the first black professional football player in 1946?

1304. What running back became the first African American to play for the University of Alabama?

1305. For what team did the first black pro football player run?

1306. When did the first black play for Paul (Bear) Bryant at the University of Alabama?

1307. Who was the first player to be drafted out of high school in National Basketball Association history?

1308. In 1962 he became the first black player to enter the Baseball Hall of Fame.

1309. A pitcher in the Negro Baseball League for 25 years, developer of the bat-badger, jumpball, and drooper, he was elected to the Baseball Hall of Fame in 1971.

1310. What player received the distinction of being named Most Valuable Player in both baseball leagues?

1311. What American League baseball team appointed the first black manager in the sport's history in 1974?

1312. Name the African American who was the first director of physical education for Harvard University.

1303. Kenny Washington	*1308.* Jackie Robinson
1304. Wilbur Jackson	*1309.* Satchel Paige
1305. Los Angeles Rams	*1310.* Frank Robinson
1306. 1971	*1311.* Cleveland Indians
1307. Daryl Dawkins	*1312.* A. Moineaux Hewlett

1313. Not recruited by Coach Bud Wilkinson, he earned an athletic scholarship and became the first African American on Oklahoma University's football team.

1314. Who organized the first black baseball team composed of waiters and bellhops in 1865?

1315. Who became the first black captain of a predominantly white football team at Massachusetts State in 1905?

1316. A home-run hitting shortstop, he became the first National League player to win the Most Valuable Player award two years in succession.

1317. What catcher reportedly hit 80 home runs in one season for the Homestead Grays?

1318. A pitcher for the Brooklyn Dodgers, he won 17 games in his rookie year.

1319. What Los Angeles Laker scored 71 points against the New York Knickerbockers?

1320. He was the first black scout for the National Basketball Association.

1321. Rated the greatest bantamweight of all time, he was a champion for 11 years.

1322. Consider the greatest welterweight of all time, he was the oldest to win the heavyweight crown.

1313. Prentice Gault   *1318.* Don Newcombe

1314. Jim Jeffries   *1319.* Elgin Baylor

1315. William Craighead   *1320.* Earl Hayes

1316. Ernie Banks   *1321.* George Dixon

1317. Josh Gibson   *1322.* Jersey Joe Walcott

1323. He knocked out more opponents than any other man in boxing.

1324. Who was the dominant featherweight champion in three divisions at once?

1325. What black man was the first American to fight for the heavyweight championship of the world against Tom Crib in 1810?

1326. Louisiana lightweight Andy Bowen fought the longest boxing contest in history, lasting how many rounds?

1327. This jockey won the first running of the Futurity in 1888.

1328. In the first Kentucky Derby running in 1875, how many of the 15 jockeys were black?

1329. Who was the first American jockey to shorten his stirup in the famed crouch position?

1330. Name the black bicycle club formed in 1892 in New York City.

1331. Who was the first black to gain admission to the U.S. Lawn Tennis Men's Singles Championship?

1332. Who was the first black Olympian?

1333. In 1916 he equaled the world record in the 440-yard dash while at the University of Chicago.

1323. Archie Moore

1324. Henry Armstrong

1325. George Dixon

1326. 110

1327. Pike Barnes

1328. 14

1329. Willie Simms

1330. The Calmuet Wheelman

1331. Reginald S. Weir

1332. George C. Poag

1333. Bingo Dismond

1334. She was the first woman to win three Olympic gold medals.

1335. He was the first black to play basketball for the University of Houston.

1336. How old was Jersey Joe Walcott when he won the heavyweight boxing championship in 1951?

1337. How many rounds was the first fight between African-American Tom Molineaux and Tom Crib last?

1338. This champion cyclist invented a steel bicycle rim.

1339. In what year were the first Negro League blacks inducted into baseball's Hall of Fame?

1340. Who was the dominant featherweight champion during the 1950s?

1341. How many lifetime homeruns did Willie Mays hit?

1342. Who broke O. J. Simpson's single-season NFL rushing record in 1984?

1343. Who set the 1987 NFL record for scoring the most touchdowns in one season?

1344. This Los Angeles Rams receiver caught passes for a league record of 336 yards in one game in 1989.

1334. Wilma Rudolph

1335. Elvin Hayes

1336. 37

1337. 44

1338. Marshall "Moyor" Taylor

1339. 1971

1340. Sandy Saddler

1341. 660

1342. Eric Dickerson

1343. Jerry Rice

1344. Willie "Flipper" Anderson

1345. This quarterback guided the NFC to victory in the 1989 Pro Bowl.

1346. Which Chicago Bears' linebacker was voted NFC Defensive Player of the Year in 1988 and became a College Football Hall of Famer in 1995?

1347. Who won the NFC Rookie of the Year award while playing for the Tampa Bay Bucs in 1991?

1348. This Edmonton Eskimos quarterback was named the Most Outstanding Player in the Canadian Football League in 1989.

1349. Which Ohio State player was the UPF College Basketball Player of the Year in 1992?

1350. Who sank the game-winning basket for Indiana University in the 1987 NCAA Championship game?

1351. This Louisville player was MVP of the 1986 NCAA Final Four and became the NBA's first draft pick three months later.

1352. Who led the Bradley College basketball team in scoring during the 1988 season?

1353. Now general manager of the New Jersey Nets, he was a Hall of Fame player for the New York Knicks in the late 1960s and early 1970s.

1345. Randall Cunningham

1346. Mike Singletary

1347. Lawrence Dawsey

1348. Tracy Ham

1349. Jim Jackson

1350. Keith Smart

1351. Pervis Ellison

1352. Hersey Hawkins

1353. Willis Reed

1354. He scored 72 points in one game, the U.S. International, during the 1991 season.

1355. He led the NCAA in assists for the 1988 season, then went on to star for the San Antonio Spurs of the NBA.

1356. Which UNLV player won the NCAA Defensive Player of the Year award in 1989, 1990, and 1991?

1357. In 1991 this Big Ten coach from Ohio State was named Associated Press Coach of the Year.

1358. From Tennessee, she was the Most Outstanding Player in women's college basketball in 1987.

1359. He led the Los Angeles Lakers in scoring in the 1991–92 season.

1360. This Boston Celtics coach won two championships in 1984 and 1986.

1361. Which New York Knicks player was the NBA's Rookie of the Year in 1988?

1362. This Houston Rockets coach was the NBA Coach of the Year in 1991.

1363. Which Negro League third baseman was named to the Baseball Hall of Fame in 1987?

1354. Kevin Bradshaw   1359. James Worthy

1355. Avery Johnson   1360. K. C. Jones

1356. Stacy Augmon   1361. Mark Jackson

1357. Randy Ayers   1362. Don Chaney

1358. Tonya Edwards   1363. Ray Dandridge

1364. Which Minnesota Twins player reached the 3,000 hit plateau playing for his hometown team in 1994?

1365. He reached 3,000 hits in 1995 and is the grand slam home run leader among active players.

1366. Who holds the 1968 single game record of twenty-one for most assists by a center?

1367. He won the MVP award at the 1987 All Star Game.

1368. This three-time Super Bowl champion player returned to his Florida alma mater to receive his bachelor's degree in 1996.

1369. Which female basketball legend was named to the Basketball Hall of Fame in 1992?

1370. One of the all-time great running backs, he was also an All-American lacrosse player at Syracuse University.

1371. This Kansas City Chiefs' linebacker was elected to the Pro Football Hall of Fame in 1986.

1372. She won a gold medal in the 1992 Olympics for the heptathlon.

1373. He led the 1992 U.S. Olympic baseball team in hitting and went on to play professionally with the Baltimore Orioles.

1364. Dave Winfield

1365. Eddie Murray

1366. Wilt Chamberlain

1367. Tim Raines

1368. Emmitt Smith

1369. Lucy Harris

1370. Jim Brown

1371. Willie Lanier

1372. Jackie Joyner-Kersee

1373. Jeffrey Hammonds

1374. Who led the 1992 U.S. Olympic basketball team in assists?

1375. Which boxer won a gold medal in the bantamweight division of the 1992 Olympics?

1376. This Canadian boxer won a gold medal in the 1992 Olympics as a heavyweight.

1377. He won the gold medal in the 110-meter hurdles in 1984 and again in 1988.

1378. She won the gold medal in the 1992 Olympics for the 200-meter dash.

1379. He broke Bob Beamon's long jump record in Japan.

1380. Which tennis player won the 1992 U.S. Clay Court Championship?

1381. He was the Major League's top home run hitter in 1987.

1382. In 1990 this slugger became the last player to hit 50 home runs in a season.

1383. He won six consecutive National League stolen base titles, starting in 1985.

1384. Who won the American League stolen base title in 1987?

1385. This Atlanta Braves' third baseman won the 1991 NL MVP award.

1386. This UNLV running back was college football's leading rusher in 1987.

1387. He was Notre Dame's last Heisman Trophy winner in 1987.

1388. Which Syracuse player won the Maxwell Award as the best quarterback in college football for 1987?

1389. This former Notre Dame star led Toronto to the 1991 Canadian Football League championship.

1390. This UCLA forward scored 30 points and 17 rebounds to help the Bruins to the 1995 NCAA title.

1391. Who won the MVP award in the first-ever rookie game during the NBA's 1994 All Star Weekend?

1392. This former Atlanta Falcons' defensive back is now a full-time baseball player.

1393. Who are the only father and son duo to win All Star MVP awards in baseball?

1394. He became the fifth player in history to record one hundred RBIs in his first five big league seasons.

1385. Terry Pendleton

1386. Ickey Woods

1387. Tim Brown

1388. Don McPherson

1389. Rocket Ismail

1390. Ed O'Bannon

1391. Anfernee Hardaway

1392. Brian Jordan

1393. Ken Griffey Jr and Sr

1394. Frank Thomas

1395. Her brother. a player with the Baltimore Orioles, may be more famous, but she was named MVP of 1994 Women's Baseball League.

1396. His career punting average of 43 yards is among the NFL's top ten in all-time history.

1397. Which St. Louis Cardinal won his eighth straight Golden Glove Award and stole 43 bases in 1987?

1398. This outfielder set the rookie record for stolen bases in 1992.

1399. This senior PGA pro recorded 13 Top Ten finishes in the 1991 season.

1400. He won $65,000 on the Senior Tour at the age of sixty-nine in 1991.

1401. Who ended his career in 1995 with the record for most free throws in NBA history?

1402. Which NBA Hall of Famer now serves as general manager of the Los Angeles Clippers?

1403. Who was the only player in the National Basketball Association history ranked in the top ten in both blocks and steals in 1995?

1404. Who set the NBA record with thirteen three-point field goals in one game during the 1995–96 season?

1395. Sheila Bonilla
1396. Reggie Roby
1397. Ozzie Smith
1398. Kenny Lofton
1399. Jim Dent

1400. Charlie Sifford
1401. Moses Malone
1402. Elgin Baylor
1403. Hakeem Olajuwon
1404. Dennis Scott

1405. He was the NFL's number one draft pick in 1991.

1406. This Reds player became only the eighteenth player in history to hit grand slam homers in back-to-back games in 1996.

1407. Which former Detroit Lions' cornerback was named to the Hall of Fame in 1992?

1408. In 1989, this Chicago White Sox player became one of only three active players to have his number retired by a team.

1409. He stole an American League record of 40 consecutive bases without being caught in 1995.

1410. He was the only major-league player ever to play with an artificial hip.

1411. This Colts player carried the ball 388 times for a club record in 1988.

1412. He was the first Olympian boxer to stop his opponent after trailing on points in 1996.

1413. This Lions player is the club's all-time leading receiver and now serves as a receivers' coach.

1414. Who became the NFL's all-time leader in kickoff returns during the 1994 season?

1405. Russell Maryland	*1410.* Bo Jackson
1406. Eric Davis	*1411.* Eric Dickerson
1407. Lem Barney	*1412.* David Reid
1408. Harold Baines	*1413.* Charlie Sanders
1409. Tim Raines	*1414.* Mel Gray

1415. This USC graduate led the Lions in passing in 1990, 1992, and 1993.

1416. Which Oakland A's pitcher won twenty games each season from 1987 to 1990?

1417. He won an American League batting title in 1989.

1418. In 1995 who tied a major-league record for home runs in the month of September?

1419. He tied a modern major-league record with three triples in a game during the 1995 season.

1420. He holds the record for most leadoff home runs in one season, with an average of twelve.

1421. Who was the American League Manager of the Year in 1989?

1422. This Georgetown University player finished fourth in the Big East Conference for scoring during his 1994–95 freshman year.

1423. He set the Big East record for points in one game by scoring 43 points for Boston College in a 1989 game.

1424. He became the NBA's only Haitian-born player in 1987.

1415. Rodney Peete

1416. Dave Stewart

1417. Kirby Puckett

1418. Albert Belle

1419. Lance Johnson

1420. Bobby Bonds

1421. Frank Robinson

1422. Alan Iverson

1423. Dana Barros

1424. Olden Polynice

1425. This New York Knick spent one of his college summers as an intern for United States Senator Bob Dole.

1426. Who is the NBA's all-time leader in playoff field goal percentage?

1427. Which Miami Hurricanes coach was the 1994–95 Big East Basketball Coach of the Year?

1428. This Cleveland Indians first baseman retired in 1987 to become a minister.

1429. In 1993 he managed the San Francisco Giants to 103 victories, which was not enough to beat the Atlanta Braves in the National League West race.

1430. Who led the majors in strikeouts in his first two seasons with the New York Mets?

1431. Whose number 29 was retired by the Minnesota Twins in 1987?

1432. This Hall of Famer's number was retired first by the Yankees in 1993.

1433. Known more for his rifle arm in right field, this Toronto Blue Jay won the American League home run title in 1986.

1434. Who won three consecutive RBI titles in the American League from 1990–92?

1425. Patrick Ewing

1426. Otis Thorpe

1427. Leonard Hamilton

1428. Andre Thornton

1429. Dusty Baker

1430. Dwight Gooden

1431. Rod Carew

1432. Reggie Jackson

1433. Jesse Barfield

1434. Cecil Fielder

1435. Who played more games for the Toronto Blue Jays than any other player?

1436. He is the Seattle Mariners' all-time leader in games played, at-bats, hits, doubles, total bases and RBIs.

1437. Who is the Kansas City Royals' all-time leader in stolen bases?

1438. He has played in the majors for just five years as of 1996, and is already seventh on the active list of American League career stolen base leaders.

1439. The first black to play in the American League, he now serves as a Special Assistant to the league President, Gene Budig.

1440. Who hit in thirty consecutive games for the Cubs in 1989?

1441. He became the only unanimous selection to the 1989 NBA All Rookie First Team, and played on the 1988 and 1996 U.S. Olympic basketball teams.

1442. Who set a record for most minutes played in an NBA finals game in 1993?

1443. He spent the first eight years of his career in Philadelphia but didn't win an NBA MVP award until he was traded to a team in the Western Conference.

1435. Lloyd Moseby

1436. Alvin Davis

1437. Willie Wilson

1438. Kenny Lofton

1439. Larry Doby

1440. Jerome Walton

1441. Mitch Richmond

1442. Kevin Johnson

1443. Charles Barkley

1444. Who was the first NBA player to garner more than one million votes in fan balloting for the 1986 All Star game?

1445. This world class shot-putter at UCLA went on to earn Super Bowl rings as a nose tackle with the San Francisco 49ers.

1446. This 49er caught the game-winning pass in Super Bowl XXIII.

1447. In 1993 he set an NFL record for most games played by an offensive lineman in a career with 246 games.

1448. Who was the first player picked by the Orlando Magic expansion in the 1989 draft?

1449. Who won the NBA Defensive Player of the Year and Most Improved Player Awards in 1986?

1450. This former (1987) NBA Rookie of the Year was named after the lead character in the 1960s TV Series, *The Rifleman.*

1451. This 20-year-old, three-time U.S. Amateur champion turned professional golfer in 1996.

1452. One of only three players to lead the NBA in scoring at least four times, he was inducted into the Basketball Hall of Fame in 1996.

1444. Magic Johnson
1445. Michael Carter
1446. John Taylor
1447. Jackie Slater
1448. Nick Anderson

1449. Alvin Robertson
1450. Chuck Person
1451. Tiger Woods
1452. George Gervin

1453. Which NBA star became the only player in history to score 2,000 or more points in nine consecutive seasons?

1454. He retired in 1986 with the major-league record for twenty pinch-hit home runs.

1455. Who set an American League record by getting hit by thirty-five pitches in one season?

1456. He set a 1986 record for most steals by a player with thirty or more home runs in one season.

1457. Who set a record for shortstops by winning his ninth Gold Glove award in 1989?

1458. Who became the first to collect one hundred RBIs for three different teams in as many seasons?

1459. Who set a record with seven consecutive hits in the 1990 World Series?

1460. Who won the Ladies World Figure Skating Championship in 1986?

1461. At the age of twenty, she cracked the Top Ten rankings on the women's pro tennis tour in 1996.

1462. Which Georgia player was named Naismith Player of the Year in women's college basketball for 1995–96?

1463. In 1991 he joined Willie Mays and Bobby Bonds as the only players to post back-to-back seasons in which he recorded thirty home runs and thirty stolen bases.

1464. Whose dramatic home run in game six won the 1993 World Series for Toronto?

1465. In 1962 at the age of nineteen, he was named MVP of the American Basketball Association.

1466. This 5 foot 7 guard won the NBA's Slam Dunk Contest in 1986.

1467. In 1987 he became the first player in thirteen years to be named MVP of the NCAA tournament and College Player of the Year.

1468. He played at Wisconsin Stevens-Point, but later became an NBA star with the Portland Trailblazers.

1469. He was drafted second in 1984s NBA draft, behind Hakeem Olajuwon and ahead of Michael Jordan.

1470. Who coached his Arkansas team to the 1994 NCAA basketball championship viewed by President Bill Clinton?

1471. Which two athletes have graced the cover of *Sports Illustrated* magazine more times than anyone?

1472. He became a Cincinnati city councilman upon retirement from football.

1463. Ron Gant

1464. Joe Carter

1465. Connie Hawkins

1466. Spud Webb

1467. Danny Manning

1468. Terry Porter

1469. Sam Bowie

1470. Nolan Richardson

1471. Muhammad Ali and Michael Jordan

1472. Reggie Williams

1473. Who was the *Sports Illustrated* Sportsman of the Year in 1992?

1474. The Dallas Cowboys traded him to Minnesota, and used the draft picks they received to build a Super Bowl team.

1475. Whose stunning knockout of Mike Tyson in Japan shocked the sports world?

1476. This pro bowler finished thirty-fifth in earnings on the PBA tour in 1989.

1477. This defensive back went to the Pro Bowl for ten of his twelve seasons with San Francisco.

1478. He topped 1,000 receiving yards six times with the Miami Dolphins.

1479. This Harvard graduate serves as studio host for Fox TV's NFL Sunday coverage.

1480. His two-run home run brought the Boston Red Sox back from the brink of elimination in the 1986 American League Championship series.

1481. Which former Chicago Cub served as honorary captain for the National League in the 1987 All Star game?

1482. She reached the finals in women's doubles at the 1992 French Open.

1473. Arthur Ashe   *1478.* Mark Clayton
1474. Herschel Walker   *1479.* James Brown
1475. Buster Douglas   *1480.* Dave Henderson
1476. Curtis Odom   *1481.* Billy Williams
1477. Ronnie Lott   *1482.* Lori McNeil

1483. Who reached the quarterfinals in women's doubles at the Australian and French Open in 1992, then went on to play Team Tennis with the Newport Beach Dukes?

1484. He retired in 1987 as the San Diego Chargers all-time leader in pass receptions with 750 receptions.

1485. Which NFL player recorded three of the top four combined yardage games in NFL history while playing with San Diego in 1985?

1486. Which NBA player holds the Houston Rockets' team record by scoring forty points or more in a game twenty-five times?

1487. He became head coach of the Tampa Bay Bucs in 1996.

1488. Which Chicago Bears superstar retired in 1987 and turned his attention toward auto racing?

1489. Which Cleveland Browns star retired in 1990 as the team's all-time leading receiver?

1490. Drafted number one by the Houston Oilers in 1978, he was elected to the Hall of Fame twelve years later.

1491. Which Giants player was the MVP of Super Bowl XXV?

1492. She was the star at the 1994 U.S. Gymnastics championships, winning five events, including All Around.

1483. Katrina Adams
1484. Charlie Joiner
1485. Lionel James
1486. Elvin Hayes
1487. Tony Dungy

1488. Walter Payton
1489. Ozzie Newsome
1490. Earl Campbell
1491. Ottis Anderson
1492. Dominique Dawes

1493. Name the NBA player whose father Calvin starred as a running back for the Dallas Cowboys in the 1970s.

1494. Who won the 1994 NCAA indoor title in the pole vault?

1495. He wrote *Slugging it Out in Japan*, a 1991 book about his years playing for the Yomiuri Giants.

1496. He was at one time the tallest player in NBA history, and set a record for blocked shots in a single season with 247 shots.

1497. Who retired in 1987, having played in the playoffs every season of his NBA career?

1498. These two former Boston Celtic greats are two of only three individuals to have played in the NCAA title game and coached an NBA championship team.

1499. Who were the first two blacks to play on an NBA championship team for the 1954–55 Syracuse Nationals?

1500. Who were the two NBA players to win the MVP award as rookies?

1501. He is the all-time saves leader in baseball.

1502. Who is the NBA's shortest player?

1493. Grant Hill

1494. Lawrence Johnson

1495. Warren Cromartie

1496. Manute Bol

1497. Julius "Dr J" Erving

1498. Bill Russell and K. C. Jones

1499. Earl Lloyd and Jim Tucker

1500. Wilt Chamberlain and Wes Unseld

1501. Lee Smith

1502. Muggsy Bogues

1503. Which two NBA players scored forty or more points a league-high eleven times each in the 1990–91 season?

1504. He led the NBA in the combined (3,619) stats of rebounds, assists and points in 1990–91.

1505. Who retired in the 1980s with more than 25,000 points scored, and starred in the movie, *Amazing Grace and Chuck?*

1506. Which Alabama player holds the 1989 NCAA record for total offensive yards in one game?

1507. This NC Central quarterback, nicknamed "Air," amassed more than 10,000 yards in career offense from 1985–88.

1508. Which Texas A&I running back won three consecutive Harlon Hill trophies as the top player in Division II football from 1987–89?

1509. Which NFL player is the career leader in touchdown catches in the professional ranks and in college?

1510. Who holds the Super Bowl single game rushing record?

1511. Which Grambling coach's team lost a 59–56 thriller in the Division I-AA football championship game in 1989?

1512. Willie Totten and Jerry Rice were the NCAA's most prolific offensive machines at this university.

1513. Scottie Pippen of the Chicago Bulls played college ball at this small school in the South.

1514. Anthony Thompson won the Maxwell Award as college football's top running back for 1989 while playing for this university.

1515. Napoleon McCallum, an NFL running back, came from which service academy?

1516. Which South Dakota State player holds the college football record for most rushing touchdowns in a single game by a freshman, in 1991?

1517. This Northern Illinois player set the 1990 NCAA record for most (308) rushing yards gained by a quarterback in one game.

1518. Isiah Thomas became general manager of what NBA expansion team in the mid-1990s?

1519. This former New York Knicks and University of Wisconsin coach became general manager of the Vancouver Grizzlies.

1520. He was the only player from a service academy to lead the NCAA in rebounding in 1986.

1521. Who was the first black golfer to win a major tournament?

1513. Central Arkansas   *1518.* Toronto Raptors

1514. Indiana University   *1519.* Stu Jackson

1515. Navy   *1520.* David Robinson

1516. Marshall Faulk   *1521.* Charles Sifford

1517. Stacey Robinson

1522. He helped turn the fortunes of the NFL's Minnesota Vikings after becoming coach in the early 1990s.

1523. He was MVP in baseball's National League in 1995.

1524. He plays for the Indiana Pacers, and his sister is coach of the USC Trojans.

1525. Whose total of 284 wins made him the best black pitcher of all-time?

1526. This NBA star released his autobiography, *Bad As I Wanna Be,* in 1996.

1527. After throwing for more than 14,000 yards at Alcorn State, he was the Houston Oilers' number-one draft pick in 1995.

1528. He is the only player in NFL history to amass 10,000 rushing yards and 5,000 receiving yards in a career.

1529. Boxer Azumah Nelson, who won the WBC super featherweight title in 1995 at the age of thirty-seven, is from which African country?

1530. Who broke Emmitt Smith's all-time University of Florida's rushing record in 1995?

1531. Who won the 1995 Heisman Trophy?

1532. This Nebraska quarterback started all but four games during a three-year undefeated stretch of regular season games for the Huskers.

1522. Dennis Green

1523. Barry Larkin

1524. Reggie and Cheryl Miller

1525. Ferguson Jenkins

1526. Dennis Rodman

1527. Steve Mcnair

1528. Marcus Allen

1529. Ghana

1530. Eric Rhett

1531. Eddie George

1532. Tommy Frazier

Entertainment

1533. Nicknamed "Leadbelly," this one-time inmate of Louisiana's notorious Angola penitentiary sang and composed work songs.

1534. This New Orleans jazz pianist, Ferdinand Joseph la Menthe Morton, won international fame under what nickname?

1535. The subject of a popular blues song, this street in the red-light district of New Orleans is commonly thought of as the birthplace of jazz.

1536. Credited with having popularized gospel music as a modern art form, she first attracted national attention through her association with Martin Luther King Jr.

1537. Released in 1920, "Crazy Blues" established this singer as the first commercially successful blues vocalist.

1538. What lame stablehand from Louisville served as inspiration for a blackface character created by Thomas Dartmouth Rice in the 1820s?

1533. Huddie Ledbetter

1534. Jelly Roll Morton

1535. Basin Street

1536. Mahalia Jackson

1537. Mamie Smith

1538. Jim Crow

1539. Who is one of the early influences on rock 'n roll, the Father of the Delta Blues?

1540. This ragtime composer wrote the opera, *Treemonisha*, which was performed only once, in 1915.

1541. He is credited with establishing a "boogie woogie" bass line still used frequently today.

1542. Duke Ellington first won recognition playing at this Harlem nightclub.

1543. What pianist's 1939 appearance with the Benny Goodman Orchestra marked the beginning of the desegregation of jazz music?

1544. After a leg injury ended his professional boxing aspirations, this soul singer formed a music group known as the Famous Flames.

1545. Originally prominent as a pianist, this pop singer also portrayed W.C. Handy in the film, *St. Louis Blues*.

1546. In May 1965 the Pulitzer Prize Advisory Board voted against honoring this bandleader, composer, and pianist.

1547. "Amateur Night" at this Harlem theater launched the careers of both Ella Fitzgerald and Billie Holiday.

1539. Robert Johnson   *1544.* James Brown

1540. Scott Joplin   *1545.* Nat "King" Cole

1541. Jimmy Yancy   *1546.* Duke Ellington

1542. The Cotton Club   *1547.* Apollo Theatre

1543. Teddy Wilson

1548. Harlem's main "jump joint" during the 1920s, this segregated club was famous for its singing and dancing black waiters.

1549. A distinctly Harlem entertainment, this type of gathering served as an alternative to segregated nightclubs for Harlem residents.

1550. His Georgia Minstrels were the first successful all-black theatrical troupe.

1551. Billed as "The Minstrel King," this popular entertainer claimed to have "the largest mouth in the world."

1552. Dan Emmet's play, *Dixie*, was first performed on April 4, 1859, in what city?

1553. This 1902 musical comedy, starring Bert Williams and George Walker, was the first successful black production that deviated from the minstrel format.

1554. Organized in 1914, this Harlem company staged all-black performances of such plays as *Dr. Jekyll and Mr. Hyde* and the *Count of Monte Cristo.*

1555. Flournoy Miller and Aubrey Lyle's musical, *Runnin' Wild*, created a sensation when it opened in 1924 by introducing what popular dance?

1556. His score for the 1929 musical, *Hot Chocolates,* included the hit, "Ain't Misbehavin'."

1548. Sugar Cane Club

1549. The rent party

1550. Charles Callender

1551. Billy Kersands

1552. New York City

1553. *In Dahomey*

1554. The Lafayette Players

1555. Charleston

1556. Fats Waller

1557. Three of his plays — *The Rider of Dreams, Granny Maumee, and Simon the Cyrenian* — were staged at Broadway's Garden Theatre in 1917.

1558. Although she first won acclaim as a jazz singer, she is best remembered for her films, including *The Sound and the Fury,* and *The Member of the Wedding.*

1559. Born in Pittsburgh in 1914, he became the first African-American pop idol, often scoring with such hits as "Tenderly," "I Apologize," and "No One but You."

1560. Mentor to Bessie Smith and known as the "Mother of the Blues," Gertrude Malissa Pridgett became famous under what name?

1561. Born Ruth Jones in Tuscaloosa, Alabama, she was later nicknamed "The Queen."

1562. On hearing the music made by his slaves, Thomas Jefferson observed that this instrument, brought from Africa, was "proper to them."

1563. In 1757 James Fenimore Cooper described this New York holiday as filled with songs and energetic dances of African origin.

1564. According to *Paxton's Directory of 1822,* New Orleans blacks congregated on this famous square to "dance, carouse, and debauch on the Sabbath."

1557. Ridgely Torrence

1558. Ethel Waters

1559. Billy Eckstine

1560. Ma Rainey

1561. Dinah Washington

1562. The banjo

1563. Pinker Day (Pentecost Sunday)

1564. Congs Square

1565. Gaudily dressed and smart-talking, this stereotypical minstrel character served as a foil for Jim Crow.

1566. This British King took banjo lessons from James Bohee, an African-American minstrel whose company toured Europe after the Civil War.

1567. This actor, known as "the Grand Old Man of the Negro Theatre," appeared in the first all-black version of *Uncle Tom's Cabin.*

1568. In what year was the first filmed version of *Uncle Tom's Cabin* produced?

1569. This 1889 all-black musical was the first New York production to omit blackface makeup and include black women in its chorus.

1570. This 1898 musical was the first show to be organized, produced, and managed by African Americans.

1571. This celebrated poet wrote lyrics for the early black musical *Clorindy — The Origin of the Cakewalk.*

1572. Produced in Harlem's Lafayette Theatre in 1913, this musical revue was the first black entertainment to attract large white audiences.

1573. In 1918, she became the first black musician to earn the master's degree in music.

1565. Zip Coon
1566. Edward VII
1567. Sam Lucas
1568. 1915
1569. The Creole Song

1570. A Trip to Coontown
1571. Paul Lawrence Dunbar
1572. Darktown Follies
1573. Nora Douglas Holt

1574. Known as "little Blackbird," this popular musical comedy star debuted with Josephine Baker in Sissle and Blake's *Shuffle Along.*

1575. Her film credits include *Broadway Rhythm, Cabin in the Sky, Till Clouds Roll By,* and *The Wiz.*

1576. Hailed by Europeans as the embodiment of "le jazz hot," this American dancer became a star after appearing at the Folies Bergeres in Paris in 1926.

1577. In 1933, he became the first black dancer to perform at New York's Metropolitan Opera Company.

1578. He played the street singer in the 1964 European film of Brecht's *Three Penny Opera*, and sang the hit song, "Mac the Knife."

1579. The NAACP tried to stop the filming of what 1947 Disney movie because of the stereotyped character of Uncle Remus?

1580. In what year did the first formal black ballet troupe debut in New York?

1581. A scholar of West Indian dance and culture, she also originated the role of Georgia Browne in the 1940 Broadway musical, *Cabin in the Sky.*

1574. Florence Mills

1575. Lena Horne

1576. Josephine Baker

1577. Hamsley Winfield

1578. Sammy Davis Jr.

1579. Song of the South

1580. 1937

1581. Katherine Dunham

1582. Born in Texas in 1931, he appeared in numerous Broadway musicals during the 1950s, and in 1958 formed the American Dance Theatre.

1583. Premiere *danseuse* of the Metropolitan Opera Ballet from 1951 to 1954, she was the first American black ballerina.

1584. This 1954 all-black musical marked the New York debut of Alvin Ailey, Arthur Mitchell, and Carmen de Lavallade.

1585. The first black ballet dancer with the New York City Ballet, he founded the Dance Theatre of Harlem in 1970.

1586. In this year, delegates of the NAACP met for the first time with Hollywood executives to discuss pejorative racial roles and the desegregation of studio labor.

1587. In this year, *Uncle Tom's Cabin* was produced by the Thomas Edison Company and starred a white man, Edwin S. Porter, in blackface.

1588. This film, originally entitled *The Clansman*, inspired a nationwide boycott by the NAACP in 1915.

1589. This black-produced and directed film which opened in 1918 was intended as a response to Griffith's *The Birth of a Nation*.

1582. Alvin Ailey	*1586.* 1942
1583. Janet Collins	*1587.* 1902
1584. *House of Flowers*	*1588.* *The Birth of a Nation*
1585. Arthur Mitchell	*1589.* *The Birth of a Race*

1590. This actress won the first Oscar ever given to a black performer.

1591. This silent film star was known during the 1920s as "the black Valentino."

1592. His Academy Award was earned by his portrayal of a tough-talking military man in *An Officer and a Gentleman.*

1593. Among his many film roles is that of Lieutenant Lothar Zogg, an Air Force bombadier in, *Dr. Strangelove or: How I Learned to Stop Worrying and Love the Bomb.*

1594. Brock Peters played Tom Robinson, wrongfully arrested for raping a white girl in this film based on Harper Lee's novel.

1595. He became famous playing John Shaft, the Harlem private eye, during the early 1970s.

1596. Cicely Tyson plays Portia, an articulate and militant maid in this 1968 screen adaptation of a Carson McCullers's novel.

1597. Paired with Diana Ross in *Lady Sings the Blues* and *Mahogany*, he also played Scott Joplin in a 1977 fictionalized film biography.

1590. Hattie McDaniel   *1594. To Kill A Mockingbird*

1591. Lorenzo Tucker   *1595.* Richard Roundtree

1592. Louis Gosset Jr.   *1596. The Heart is a Lonely Hunter*

1593. James Earl Jones   *1597.* Billy Dee Williams

1598. This jazz trumpeter wrote dialogue and music for *The Hat*, a cartoon which depicts the origins of international conflict.

1599. This Motown producer's first screen undertaking was *Mahogany*, which he directed.

1600. Known primarily as an actress, she received a screen writing credit for *Up Tight*, a film examining the black power movement after King's death and based loosely on Liam O'Flaherty's novel, *The Informer*.

1601. He played Buckwheat in countless "Our Gang" episodes during the 1930s.

1602. She plays a Bessie Smith-style blues singer in *All the Fine Young Cannibals*, the story of a white musician's career in the jazz world.

1603. This celebrated composer and bandleader appeared as Pie Eye in Otto Preminger's *Anatomy of a Murder*.

1604. Cicely Tyson starred in this 1974 television movie, which won nine Emmys, about the fictional life of a 110-year old woman.

1605. This 1958 film featured acts from the Harlem Variety Revue at the Apollo Theatre.

1598. Dizzy Gillespie

1599. Berry Gordy Jr.

1600. Ruby Dee

1601. Billie Thomas

1602. Pearl Bailey

1603. Duke Ellington

1604. *The Autobiography of Miss Jane Pittman*

1605. *Basin Street Revue*

1606. He was famous for his "Minnie the Moocher" and performed it in 1932s *The Big Broadcast.*

1607. His first film appearance was in the 1929 movie, *Black and Tan,* where he played his "Black and Tan Fantasy."

1608. He narrated *Body and Soul: Soul, Part II,* a 1968 CBS-TV documentary of soul music in America.

1609. This Otto Preminger 1954 film adaptation of Bizet's opera stars Harry Belafonte and pianist Dorothy Dandridge.

1610. Tamara Dobson played the title role in this 1973 film of an international narcotics agent who rids drugs from the black community with good looks, karate, and aid from the community.

1611. Who is the author of *Dutchman,* about a man taunted and abused by a young white female passenger in a New York subway train?

1612. When he produced the film, *Florida Crackers,* this pioneer filmmaker included a graphic lynching scene which was a source of great controversy.

1613. At age 76, this former slave and eminent scientist narrated a 1940 documentary dramatizing his struggles and successes to a young boy pondering the options for the future.

1606. Cab Calloway

1607. Duke Ellington

1608. Ray Charles

1609. Carmen Jones

1610. Cleopatra Jones

1611. Amiri Baraka

1612. Bill Foster

1613. George Washington Carver

1614. He played himself in *The Greatest*, a 1977 film tracking this man's life from a small-town childhood, through the influence of Malcolm X, to his acceptance of the Muslim faith.

1615. Paul Winfield, Rex Ingram, Clarence Muse, silent actor George Reed, and even boxing champion Archie Moore have all played this role in various film versions of *The Adventures of Huckleberry Finn*.

1616. In the 1934 film version of *Imitation of Life*, about a light-skinned black girl who tries to pass for white, what black actress plays the girl's role?

1617. Before becoming a solo singer, he was the lead for the Temptations until 1968.

1618. They played Roy Campanella and his wife in *It's Good to be Alive*, a movie about the baseball great and his tragic, crippling car accident.

1619. There is a short dramatization of *Uncle Tom's Cabin* in this 1956 Fox musical.

1620. This former pro-footballer was later seen on TV commercials running through airports.

1621. This acclaimed singer made her film debut in the 1972 feature about blues great, Billie Holiday.

1614. Muhammad Ali

1615. Jim

1616. Fredi Washington

1617. David Ruffin

1618. Paul Winfield and Ruby Dee

1619. *The King and I*

1620. O. J. Simpson

1621. Diana Ross

1622. This jazz vocalist plays a nightclub singer hooked on drugs in the 1960 feature, *Let No Man Write My Epitaph.*

1623. Brock Peters, Melba Moore, and Raymond St. Jacques performed in this musical film version of Alan Paton's *Cry, the Beloved Country.*

1624. In the irreverent 1970 movie, M*A*S*H Fred Williamson plays an army doctor whose accomplished passing on the football field earned him this nickname.

1625. Diana Ross received an Oscar nomination for costume design for this 1975 movie.

1626. Sammy Davis Jr., Louis Armstrong, and Ossie Davis made this film in 1966, exploring the world and the inner struggles of the black jazz musician.

1627. She played the title role in the all-black Broadway version of *Hello Dolly.*

1628. She presented *Your Arms too Short to Box With God* on Broadway in the mid-1970s.

1629. Stephanie Mills recreated Judy Garland's role in this Broadway musical which was a revamping of the 1939 MGM classic.

1622. Ella Fitzgerald   *1626. A Man Called Adam*

1623. Lost in the Stars   *1627.* Pearl Bailey

1624. Spearchucker   *1628.* Vinnette Carroll

1625. Mahogany   *1629. The Wiz*

1630. They played the title roles in the 1959 film, *Porgy and Bess*.

1631. In this year ABC-TV aired its mini-series extravaganza, based on Alex Haley's book, *Roots*.

1632. In *Roots*, Kunta Kinte of the Mandika tribe is abducted into slavery in the 1750s from what is now this African nation.

1633. She played Prissy in the 1939 romance, *Gone With the Wind*.

1634. Known as one of the premier singers of romantic ballads, this vocalist originally wanted to run track in the Olympics.

1635. Turned into a vampire, William Marshall is unleashed on Los Angeles in this 1972 film.

1636. His music won an Oscar for the 1971 detective drama, *Shaft*.

1637. Gene Wilder is paired with this famous comedian in the 1976 film effort, *Silver Streak*.

1638. This choir performed in countless films in the 1930s and 1940s, including *Slave Ship*.

1639. He portrayed Fred Sanford, a lazy junk collector on TV's *Sanford and Son*.

1630. Sidney Poitier and Dorothy Dandridge
1631. 1977
1632. Gambia
1633. Butterfly McQueen
1634. Johnny Mathis
1635. *Blacula*
1636. Isaac Hayes
1637. Richard Pryor
1638. The Hall-Johnson Choir
1639. Redd Foxx

1640. In this 1972 film, a desperate Paul Winfield is sentenced to a chain gang when he steals meat for his hungry family.

1641. He was the eligible, John Prentice, who came to dinner in 1967s *Guess Who's Coming to Dinner*.

1642. Irene Cara is well known for her portrayal of Coco, a student at Manhattan's High School of Performing Arts, in this film.

1643. Ernest Morrison played this character, the first black to appear in the "Our Gang" silent films.

1644. He plays Big Daddy, with whom Shirley MacLaine falls in love in the musical film, *Sweet Charity*.

1645. She is affectionately called "Lady Day."

1646. He is famous for sporting one sequined glove and for housing a wildlife menagerie in his backyard in addition to countless hit records and videos.

1647. He wrote "Honeysuckle Rose," which Lena Horne sang in the MGM star-studded variety show, *Thousands Cheer*.

1648. Sidney Poitier teaches in a rough, London school and slowly gains his student's respect in this 1967 film.

1640. Sounder

1641. Sidney Poitier

1642. Fame

1643. Sunshine Sammy

1644. Sammy Davis Jr.

1645. Billie Holiday

1646. Michael Jackson

1647. Fats Waller

1648. To Sir With Love

1649. Said to be "the first black man to have a leading role in films," he played Tom in the 1914 silent film, *Uncle Tom's Cabin*.

1650. Richard Pryor played the first black to cross the color line in auto racing, and Pam Grier played his wife, in this 1977 film.

1651. Melville Van Peebles made his directorial debut with this 1970 film about a bigot who turns black overnight.

1652. He was George Jefferson, dry cleaning store owner, and next-door neighbor to Archie Bunker, in television's *All in the Family*.

1653. Film actor Clarence Muse wrote the screenplay with Langston Hughes and aided in the direction of this 1939 movie.

1654. The 1922 silent film, *Wife Hunters*, is one of the few all-black silents to be filmed on location in this Mississippi city.

1655. Harry Belafonte starred in this 1959 film about life after a nuclear war in New York City, where only three people have survived: a black man, a white man, and a white woman over whom they struggle.

1656. Jannie Hoskins played this lesser-known character in numerous "Our Gang" episodes.

1649. Sam Lucas

1650. Greased Lighting

1651. Watermelon Man

1652. Sherman Helmsley

1653. Way Down South

1654. Vicksburg

1655. The World, the Flesh, and the Devil

1656. Mango

1657. This Broadway star shares the screen with William Powell, Esther Williams, Judy Garland and Fred Astaire in the 1946 film, *Ziegfeld Follies*.

1658. This jazz great has performed in the films *The Glenn Miller Story, Hello, Dolly* and *Satchmo the Great*.

1659. This movie actor, director, and producer also played one of the prisoners or war in the television series, *Hogan's Heroes*.

1660. Before being known for authoring *Roots*, Alex Haley wrote the screenplay for this 1973 film.

1661. More known for performances in front of the camera, this man also worked behind the camera, directing *Buck and the Preacher* and *Uptown Saturday Night*.

1662. She started singing in the choir of her father's church, and went on to earn respect as the first lady of soul.

1663. She was in the film, *Cleopatra Jones* but is better known as the mother of a family living in the Chicago projects in *Good Times*.

1664. He performed in *Claudine*, and *Cooley High*, and was a "sweathog" for several years on the TV series, *Welcome Back, Kotter*.

1657. Avon Long

1658. Louis Armstrong

1659. Ivan Dixon

1660. *Super Fly TNT*

1661. Sidney Poitier

1662. Aretha Franklin

1663. Esther Rolle

1664. Lawrence-Hilton Jacobs

1665. He plays the talented Harlem street kid, Leroy, in the TV series and the film, *Fame*.

1666. In the 1974 film, *Claudine*, she plays a welfare mother of six.

1667. The "Midnight Train to Georgia" brought this singer fame.

1668. In *For Pete's Sake*, he co-stars with the Reverend Billy Graham.

1669. This terrific tapdancer of Broadway's *Sophisticated Ladies*, also danced in the films *The Cotton Club* and *White Nights*.

1670. Featured in the films, *Car Wash, Cooley High,* and *Where's Poppa*, he was also a member of TV's *Saturday Night Live*.

1671. In addition to writing the screenplay, she also wrote the songs featured in the 1972 film *Georgia, Georgia*.

1672. This 1954 movie starring Sidney Poitier and the Harlem Globetrotters centers on the basketball team's rise from obscurity to prominence as a major box office attraction.

1665. Gene Anthony Ray

1666. Diahann Carroll

1667. Gladys Knight

1668. Al Freeman Jr.

1669. Gregory Hines

1670. Garrett Morris

1671. Maya Angelou

1672. *Go, Man, Go*

1673. She performed in a segregated segment of the film, *Flying Down to Rio*, and sang an unforgettable rendition of the gritty song, "Remember My Forgotten Man" in *Gold Diggers of 1933*.

1674. He and his audience sing back and forth when he performs his famous scat song, "Hi-de-ho."

1675. Bill Cosby and Robert Culp play a pair of zany detectives who experience the same passions, pleasures, and vices in this 1972 film.

1676. Loretta, Niagara, Gussie, Pearl, and Willamay are just some of the countless servant's roles she played in films like 1934's *Imitation of Life*.

1677. Born in Georgia in 1932, this blind singer, composer, and pianist sang the theme song to the film, *In the Heat of the Night*.

1678. Billie Holiday was one of the first blues singers to perform here in New York City.

1679. He played *Piano Man*, Billie Holiday's faithful but weak-willed friend in *Lady Sings the Blues*.

1680. Chuck Berry, Little Richard, Chubby Checker, Bo Diddley, The Shirelles, and Fats Domino are showcased in this 1973 documentary.

1673. Etta Moten

1674. Cab Calloway

1675. Hickey and Boggs

1676. Louise Beavers

1677. Ray Charles

1678. Carnegie Hall

1679. Richard Pryor

1680. Let the Good Times Roll

1681. In this the eighth James Bond film, the villains include Yaphet Kotto, Julius Harris, and Geoffrey Holder as the voodoo prince.

1682. J. Rosamond Johnson, trained at the New England Conservatory of Music in Boston, and his brother James Weldon Johnson, wrote this popular song near the turn of the century.

1683. Marla Gibbs is well-known by TV audiences for this sassy, back-talking role on *The Jeffersons*.

1684. Paul Robeson sang this popular description of the Mississippi.

1685. This limber dancer was seen in the movie and TV series *Fame*, and danced lead roles in Broadway shows like the revival of *Sweet Charity*.

1686. His awards include the ASCAP Awards' Composer of the Year for three consecutive years.

1687. She sang Martin Luther King Jr.'s favorite gospel song, "Precious Lord, Take My Hand," after his funeral procession in 1968.

1688. In what television series did Diahann Carroll play a nurse?

1681. Live and Let Die

1682. "Lift Ev'ry Voice and Sing"

1683. Florence

1684. "Ole Man River"

1685. Debbie Allen

1686. Lionel Richie

1687. Mahalia Jackson

1688. Julia

1689. She sang "Goldfinger," "Diamonds Are Forever," and "Moonraker" for the title tracks of those James Bond films.

1690. In the early 1960s, this ex-production line worker organized the Motown recording company.

1691. In 1963, Sidney Poitier won an Oscar for his role as a traveling vagabond who befriends a group of immigrant nuns and helps them build a missionary school.

1692. Once a member of the singing duo "Dawn" which backed up Tony Orlando, she can be seen with Nell Carter on *Gim'me a Break*.

1693. Born Eleanor Fasin in Baltimore in 1915, this great vocalist recorded the hit "Lover Man" in 1944.

1694. At 16, she joined the Cotton Club as a dancer; in 1943, she performed what was to become her signature tune, "Stormy Weather."

1695. He played Harlem-born-and bred Duke Curtis in the 1964 film, *The Cool World*.

1696. Known as the "First Lady of Jazz", one of her first big breaks was singing with Chick Webb and his band at the Harlem Opera House in the mid-1930s.

1689. Shirley Bassey

1690. Berry Gordy Jr.

1691. Lilies of the Field

1692. Telma Hopkins

1693. Billie Holiday

1694. Lena Horne

1695. Clarence Williams

1696. Ella Fitzgerald

1697. Born in 1887, this concert artist broke the color bar in concert halls for black classical singers.

1698. He played Bigger Thomas in the film version of *Native Son.*

1699. She was the first female black to be cast in a major role on one of the network's prime time soap operas.

1700. This famous concert and opera singer, born in 1927, has appeared in opera houses worldwide, and received the Order of Merit of the Italian Republic.

1701. This celebrated actor on Broadway and in Hollywood was a lawyer, athlete, and leader in civil rights struggles, and a member of Phi Beta Kappa.

1702. What was the nickname of Bill Robinson, the dancer who made more than 14 Hollywood movies in the 1930s?

1703. William Grant Still, accomplished composer and conductor, was the first black to lead a symphony orchestra when he conducted this group.

1704. Known for his freestyle improvisational style, this artist was the first jazz musician to receive a Guggenheim fellowship.

1697. Roland Hayes

1698. Canada Lee

1699. Diahann Carroll

1700. Leontyne Price

1701. Paul Robeson

1702. "Bojangles"

1703. Los Angeles Philharmonic

1704. Ornette Coleman

1705. An early associate of Charlie Parker and Dizzy Gillespie and a pioneer in the use of modern choral backgrounds, this Brooklyn-born drummer co-wrote the "Freedom Now Suite."

1706. Lionel Hampton started as a drummer, led a big band until the 1960s, and has a special reputation as the first man to play jazz on this instrument.

1707. His most successful record was "Body and Soul," and he is the first prominent tenor saxophone soloist in jazz history.

1708. Affectionately called "Yardbird," this jazz great was born in Kansas City in 1920.

1709. One of the finest jazz guitarists, he became known on 52nd Street and through performances with the Washboard Rhythm Kings and the Spirits of Rhythm in the 1930s.

1710. Singing with the Raelettes (a gospel-based back-up group) in concerts, Ray Charles released this hit in 1959.

1711. In 1946, he was cast as Daniel de Bosola in the play, *The Duchess of Malfi*, becoming the first black actor to appear in New York in a previously white role.

1705. Max Roach   *1709.* Teddy Bunn
1706. Vibraharp   *1710.* "Georgia on My Mind"
1707. Coleman Hawkins   *1711.* Canada Lee
1708. Charlie Parker

1712. This pianist, with a riving, rhythmic left hand and nicknamed "The Lion," helped to establish the style known as the Harlem stride.

1713. This influential jazz pianist wrote the 1920s pop hit, "Charleston."

1714. Blues singer and guitarist, he won a pardon from a Louisiana prison for murder.

1715. This New Orleans musician was the first prominent string bass soloist on jazz recordings.

1716. This arranger and pianist composed the popular standard, "Take the 'A Train."

1717. This black actor made his film debut in the 1949 war drama, *Home of the Brave.*

1718. Billie Holiday's nickname, "Lady Day," was affectionately coined by this saxophonist.

1719. It is the singing of nonsense syllables instead of words, with the syllable phrased as if it were coming from a jazz horn instead of a voice.

1720. He forgot the lyric of a song during a recording session and thereby invented "scatting."

1712. Willie Smith

1713. James P. Johnson

1714. Huddie "Leadbelly" Ledbetter

1715. George "Pops" Foster

1716. Billy Strayhorn

1717. James Edwards

1718. Lester Young

1719. Scat singing

1720. Louis Armstrong

1721. Maryland actor Ira Aldrich, unable to get serious roles in American theatre, went to England where he performed the role of Othello on the London stage in this year.

1722. Katherine Dunham left the professional stage after tremendous success to live in the ghetto of this Illinois city to work with disadvantaged youth.

1723. After several years off the charts, she came back in the 1980s in her 40s with "What's Love Got to Do With It?"

1724. This former model sold six million copies of her debut album by 1986, making it the best-selling LP by a black female vocalist in pop music history.

1725. This world-famous "King of the Blues" averages a hectic 300 concert dates a year.

1726. This trumpeter made history by winning Grammys in both classical and jazz fields.

1727. Billy Eckstine and Carmen McRae are both seen in this 1986 Richard Pryor film.

1728. Once married to great Teddy Wilson, she was a fine pianist in her own right, and one of the few female artists to lead her own band.

1721. 1833   *1725.* B. B. King
1722. East St. Louis   *1726.* Wynton Marsalis
1723. Tina Turner   *1727.* *Jo Jo Dancer*
1724. Whitney Houston   *1728.* Irene Wilson

1729. Cannonball Adderley is a star graduate from this Florida college.

1730. This Chicago talk-show hostess won a Best Supporting Actress nomination for her portrayal of the strong-willed Sophia in *The Color Purple*.

1731. Who was the only black actress to win the Academy Award's Best Supporting Actress Oscar since Hattie McDaniel in 1939?

1732. He owns two Emmies for his co-starring role on the 1960s *I Spy* series, and was a cinch to capture the award for Best Actor in a sitcom in 1985, but withdrew his name not wanting to compete with fellow actors.

1733. This veteran rock-n-roller and evangelist discovered that his songs were often re-recorded and credited to singers like Elvis Presley or Pat Boone.

1734. Known for Broadway hits like *Ain't Supposed to Die a Natural Death*, this playwright/director/producer added options trader to his list of credits when he hit Wall Street in the 1980s.

1735. In 1939, the Daughters of the American Revolution denied this contralto permission to sing in Washington, D.C.'s Constitution Hall.

1729. Florida A&M

1730. Oprah Winfrey

1731. Whoopi Goldberg

1732. Bill Cosby

1733. Little Richard (Penniman)

1734. Melvin Van Peebles

1735. Marian Anderson

1736. In 1961, this soprano from Mississippi debuted at the Metropolitan Opera House singing Leonora in Verdi's *Il Trovatore* and received a 42-minute ovation.

1737. This trumpeter with the middle name of Toussaint L'Overture has a doctorate in ethnomusicology.

1738. Name the bassist who played with Horace Silver at 18 and made his reputation with *Chick Corea's Return to Forever*.

1739. His nickname is Jaws.

1740. Name the Mississippi Delta bluesman whose "Boogie Chillen" sold a million copies in 1948.

1741. Who is the hard-driving master drummer best known for his innovative work with John Coltrane?

1742. Blind, he would play three instruments at once.

1743. He was pianist with the John Coltrane Quartet for five years from its inception in 1960.

1744. This superb saxophonist wrote for the Jazz Messengers and Miles Davis, then formed Weather Report.

1745. Name the big-toned sax player nicknamed "Jug."

1736. Leontyne Price	*1741.* Elvin Jones
1737. Donald Byrd	*1742.* Rahsaan Roland Kirk
1738. Stanley Clarke	*1743.* McCoy Tyner
1739. Eddie "Lockjaw" Davis	*1744.* Wayne Shorter
1740. John Lee Hooker	*1745.* Gene Ammons

1746. She worked with Paul Whiteman's band between 1929–1933 and became well-known for her rendition of "Rockin' Chair."

1747. This pianist composed the funky "Moanin" and "Dat Dere" for the Jazz Messengers.

1748. His culturally relevant album, *We Insist! Freedom Now Suite* is believed to have contributed to this drummer's five-year blacklist from the recording studios in the 1960s.

1749. Name the masterly tenor saxophonist who produced the classic album, *Way Out West.*

1750. A superb composer, he co-founded the Jazz Messengers with Art Blakey.

1751. Many term him the greatest jazz violinist; his first name is Hezekiah.

1752. Born Sonny Blount, he explored exotic compositions with his Solar Arkestra.

1753. Name the group that recorded "My True Story" on the Beltone label.

1754. Name the original lead singer for the Four Tops.

1755. How many top ten records did the Supremes produce from 1964 to 1969?

1746. Mildred Bailey		*1751.* Stuff Smith
1747. Bobby Timmons		*1752.* Sun Ra
1748. Max Roach		*1753.* Jive Five
1749. Sonny Rollins		*1754.* Levi Stubbs
1750. Horace Silver		*1755.* 16

1756. Who recorded the 1960 hit, "Ooh Poo Pah Doo"?

1757. One of the pioneers of bebop, he wore outlandish hats and composed "Mysterioso."

1758. In 1963, at age 12, he recorded "Fingertips."

1759. Who recorded "Can I Change My Mind?" the 1969 hit?

1760. "I Found A Love" was recorded by the Falcons in 1962 with this singer as lead.

1761. This jazz trumpeter was born in Philadelphia and shot dead outside a New York City club, Slugs.

1762. This blues-based percussive pianist has contributed classics like "Doodlin'," "The Preacher," "Senor Blues" and "Song for My Father."

1763. Jazz's best-known organist, he recorded "A Walk on the Wild Side" for Verve.

1764. Acknowledged by many as bebop's greatest pianist, he settled in Paris in 1959 and produced *Our Man in Paris* with Dexter Gordon.

1765. In 1958, this saxophonist's composition, "The Freedom Suite" was reissued as "The Shadow Waltz" because of its reference to African-American equality.

1756. Jesse Hill

1757. Thelonious Monk

1758. Stevie Wonder

1759. Tyrone Davis

1760. Wilson Pickett

1761. Lee Morgan

1762. Horace Silver

1763. Jimmy Smith

1764. Bud Powell

1765. Sonny Rollins

1766. Name the percussion player who composed the frequently recorded "Afro-Blue."

1767. This bluesman's real name is Peter Chatman.

1768. Touted as the "Mother of the Blues," this vocalist made her first public appearance at age 12 in the vaudeville show, "Bunch of Blackberries."

1769. Who composed "I'm Just Wild About Harry," Harry Truman's 1948 presidential campaign song?

1770. This jazz singer conducted Chick Webb's orchestra after his death.

1771. What jazz pianist wrote the standard, "Misty"?

1772. What jazz trumpeter made the beret, horn-rim glasses and goatee the bebop uniform?

1773. This child prodigy performed Mozart Piano Concertos with the Chicago Symphony Orchestra at age 11.

1774. This musician was the first jazz banjoist to attain a reputation.

1775. At age 14, she toured with Ma Rainey's Rabbit Foot Minstrels.

1776. This pianist established the style known as Harlem stride.

1766. Mongo Santamaria

1767. "Memphis Slim"

1768. Ma Rainey

1769. Eubie Blake

1770. Ella Fitzgerald

1771. Errol Garner

1772. Dizzy Gillespie

1773. Herbie Hancock

1774. Johnny St. Cyr

1775. Bessie Smith

1776. Willie "The Lion" Smith

1777. What big bluesman popularized "Shake Rattle & Roll" long before Bill Haley and the Comets?

1778. She is the "Divine One."

1779. What pianist-composer-vocalist appeared in the movie, *Stormy Weather*?

1780. Because of her height and thinness, this jazz songstress was known as "Sweet Mama Stringbean."

1781. This blues guitarist-harmonica player and vocalist's real name is McKinley Morganfield.

1782. Because of her composing, arranging and piano playing, she is called the First Lady of Jazz.

1783. In the late 1930s, Billie Holiday forged a partnership with what famous sax-man?

1784. This ballad-singing group was described by Decca Records as "five boys and a guitar."

1785. The Spaniels, on the Vee Jay label, had a success with this tune in 1954.

1786. Bobby Lester sang lead for this Moonglows hit on the Chess label.

1787. Name the lead singer for most of the recordings by the Platters.

1777. Big Joe Turner

1778. Sarah Vaughan

1779. Fats Waller

1780. Ethel Waters

1781. Muddy Waters

1782. Mary Lou Williams

1783. Lester Young

1784. Mills Brothers

1785. "Goodnight Sweetheart, Goodnight"

1786. "Sincerely"

1787. Tony Williams

1788. Name the lead singer with the 'fifties rhythm and blues group, the Orioles.

1789. This singer's biggest success was "Jim Dandy."

1790. This rhythm and blues group hit it big in 1953 with their tune, "Crying in the Chapel."

1791. Who sang lead for the Five Kings on their 1951 success, "Glory of Love"?

1792. LaVern Baker's hit "Tweedle Dee" was recorded in what year?

1793. Who sang "Life is But a Dream" and "A Sunday Kind of Love"?

1794. Who sang lead for the Five Satins 1956 recording, "(I'll Remember) In the Still of the Night"?

1795. Name the big touring band which was called a "Rhythm and Blues Caravan."

1796. Who recorded "No Rollin' Blues" in 1949?

1797. Her recording of "5–10–15 Hours" in 1952 featured a tenor solo by Willis Jackson.

1798. Roy Milton's recording of this tune in 1945 was the first to reach sales of more than a million copies in the African-American market.

1788. Sonny Til

1789. LaVern Baker

1790. Orioles

1791. Rudy West

1792. 1954

1793. Harptones

1794. Fred Parris

1795. Johnny Otis Show

1796. Jimmy Witherspoon

1797. Ruth Brown

1798. "R. M. Blues"

1799. What was Ike Turner's jump band called?

1800. His first record at age 17, "The Fat Man," was one of the biggest rhythm and blues hits of 1949.

1801. His biggest hit was his first record in 1952, "Lawdy, Miss Clawdy."

1802. Name the tune by Ivory Joe Hunter which sold over a million copies in 1950.

1803. The influential "Please Send Me Someone to Love" was recorded in 1950 by whom?

1804. He was one of Aristocrat/Chess Records best-selling recording artists, releasing "Hoochie Coochie" in 1950.

1805. One of the few guitar-playing woman blues singers, she recorded the 1962 success, "You'll Lose A Good Thing."

1806. Who was the lead singer for the Drifters on "Dance With Me"?

1807. A native of Laurel, Mississippi, she began piano lessons at age four and was called the "voice of the century."

1808. This graduate of Wayne State University became the leading male singer among black operatic stars in the 1960s.

1799. Ike Turner's Kings of Rhythm
1800. Fats Domino
1801. Lloyd Price
1802. "I Almost Lost My Mind"
1803. Percy Mayfield
1804. Muddy Waters
1805. Barbara Lynn
1806. Ben E. King
1807. Leontyne Price
1808. George Shirley

1809. He was the first black man to be appointed to a permanent position as a symphony orchestra conductor in the United States in 1968.

1810. He was the first black American to conduct a white radio orchestra in the nation when he conducted WNBC's Deep River orchestra in 1930.

1811. In 1955, she became the first African-American to star in an opera on television when she appeared in Puccini's *Tosca*.

1812. He became the first African-American male to obtain a permanent association with the Metropolitan Opera.

1813. One of the first blacks to prepare for a career conducting symphony orchestras, he took a permanent position with the Goteborg Symphony in Sweden.

1814. This African-American actress was nominated for an Academy Award for her portrayal of Tina Turner in *What's Love Got to Do With It*.

1815. The leading figure of the avant garde jazz movement of the 1950s, this alto saxophonist was the first jazz musician to receive a Guggenheim Fellowship.

1816. Bandleader, arranger, composer, he wrote the score for the film, *The Pawnbroker* and for the television series, *Ironside*.

1809. Henry Lewis

1810. William Grant Still

1811. Leontyne Price

1812. George Shirley

1813. Dean Dixon

1814. Angela Bassett

1815. Ornette Coleman

1816. Oliver Nelson

1817. In 1954, the first jazz festival in the United States was held in this town.

1818. A pioneer principal black singer for the New York City Opera Company in 1946, he sang in Leoncavallo's *Pagliacci*.

1819. Who recorded the top ten hits, "This Magic Moment" and "Save the Last Dance For Me" in 1960?

1820. Three top black ballad singers died violently in the 1960s — Johnny Ace, Sam Cooke and this man.

1821. Formerly with the Pilgrim Travellers, he sang a duet with Sam Cooke on "Bring it on Home to Me."

1822. Name the gospel-influenced ballad singer of the 'fifties who would tear off his clothes for his audience.

1823. He recorded the first rhythm and blues rendition of "Unclaimed Melody" in 1955.

1824. Name the Drifters' first recorded song.

1825. "Work With Me, Annie" was recorded by what group?

1826. "Please, Please, Please" was the big hit by James Brown and the Famous Flames in what year?

1817. Newport, R. I.

1818. Todd Duncan

1819. Drifters

1820. Jesse Belvin

1821. Lou Rawls

1822. Jackie Wilson

1823. Roy Hamilton

1824. "Money Honey"

1825. Midnighters

1826. 1956

1827. The twist dance style was conceived by this singer whose recordings of the same name sold more than a million copies in the black community.

1828. Who recorded "A Million to One" in 1961?

1829. The Five Blind Boys of Mississippi recorded for what Houston-based record label?

1830. Who was the lead singer for the Dominoes for their hit, "The Bells"?

1831. Who wrote "Got a Job" and "Bad Girls" for the Miracles?

1832. Clyde McPhatter left the Dominoes to form this group.

1833. She was lead singer in the all-woman vocal group, the Shirelles.

1834. On what label did the Miracles record "Shop Around" in 1961?

1835. Who recorded "Daddy's Home" in 1961?

1836. In 1957, Juggy Murray formed this record company which released songs by Ike and Tina Turner.

1837. This group was the most commercially successful of all Motown entertainers.

1838. What is Sly Stone's real name?

1827. Chubby Checker
1828. Jimmy Charles
1829. Peacock
1830. Clyde McPhatter
1831. Smokey Robinson
1832. Drifters

1833. Shirley Owens
1834. Tamla
1835. Shep and the Limelites
1836. Sue Records
1837. Supremes
1838. Sylvester Stewart

1839. How many songs did Fats Domino have on the rhythm and blues top ten lists during the 1955–60 period?

1840. Their 1986 rap album, *Licensed to Kill*, sold an unprecedented four million copies in the U.S.

1841. Which organization hosted the premiere of Spike Lee's *She Gotta Have It* in 1986?

1842. Who wrote the *Colored Museum* which opened at New York's Public Theater in 1986?

1843. James Earl Jones starred in this 1987 August Wilson play that won a Pulitzer Prize.

1844. His satire on Hollywood's mistreatment of blacks, *Hollywood Shuffle*, was a major motion picture statement in 1987.

1845. Name the 1986 opera about Malcolm X composed by Anthony Davis with a libretto by Thulani Davis.

1846. Tim Reid starred in and co-produced this 1987 sitcom about black Southerners.

1847. Her single, "Fast Car," is also the title of her 1988 album.

1848. He offered the Mothership Connection of funk music in 1976.

1839. 24

1840. The Beastie Boys

1841. The Black Filmmaker Foundation

1842. George Wolfe

1843. *Fences*

1844. Robert Townsend

1845. X

1846. *Frank's Place*

1847. Tracy Chapman

1848. George Clinton

1849. Who wrote the musical score for the 1976 movie, *Sparkle?*

1850. Which double album released by Stevie Wonder in 1976 represents a new departure for black love songs?

1851. What is the title of Al Green's first hit in 1971?

1852. A co-founder of bepop, this jazz trumpeter died in 1993.

1853. The 1929 movie *Hallelujah* starred this black actress.

1854. For what song did Luther Vandross win a Grammy Award in 1990 for Best Male Vocalist for rhythm and blues?

1855. Their top hit in 1972 was "Papa Was a Rolling Stone."

1856. In 1989, he won an Academy Award for Best Supporting Actor in *Glory.*

1857. What honor did Pearl Bailey receive in 1988 from the White House?

1858. The NAACP named her Entertainer of the Year in 1985.

1859. He was drummer for the Duke Ellington band for 30 years.

1860. He secured his place as the Ambassador of Love with his 1995 single, "Practice What You Preach."

1849. Curtis Mayfield

1850. *Songs in the Key of Life*

1851. "Tired of Being Alone"

1852. Dizzy Gillespie

1853. Nina Mae McKinney

1854. "Here and Now"

1855. Temptations

1856. Denzel Washington

1857. Presidential Medal of Freedom

1858. Patti LaBelle

1859. Sonny Greer

1860. Barry White

1861. This 1972 film about cocaine dealing stars Ron O'Neal with a score by Curtis Mayfield.

1862. Whose widow started Revenge Records, releasing recordings by her famous bassist husband that were available in 1996 only on bootleg editions?

1863. This alto saxist was a soloist for James Brown and George Clinton as well as being a Famous Flame.

1864. In 1912 he was responsible for the first jazz concert at Carnegie Hall, featuring 125 instruments and 10 pianos.

1865. Who developed the style known as swing, featuring call-and-response patterns, extensive use of the riff — the repetition of a motif — and the frequent insertion of improvised solos?

1866. Who developed with Bennie Moten the Kansas City swing style that emphasized a blues motif, tempos of breakneck speed, and a breathtaking use of riffs?

1867. Her middle name was Freda, and this dancer and jazz singer was called the Black Venus.

1868. Who was the great tenor saxophonist called Bean?

1869. This first Hollywood exploitation film was directed by Gordon Park Sr. in 1971.

1861. Superfly
1862. Charlie Mingus
1863. Maceo Parker
1864. James Reese Europe
1865. Fletcher Henderson
1866. Count Basie
1867. Josephine Baker
1868. Coleman Hawkins
1869. Shaft.

1870. His debut solo release, *Black Art*, became one of the most critically acclaimed jazz records of 1994, and was chosen one of the top ten jazz CD's of the year by the *New York Times*.

1871. Which composer during the first decade of the century insisted, "I am not the world's greatest Negro violinist. I am the world's greatest violinist."?

1872. He sang with New Edition before his solo hit, "My Prerogative," in 1988.

1873. Ike and Tina Turner are highlighted in this 1971 documentary.

1874. Marvin Gaye wrote the score for this 1972 film starring Robert Hooks.

1875. *Enter the Dragon*, Bruce Lee's 1973 low-budget film, featured this black martial artist as costar.

1876. Harlem drug chieftain Nicky Barnes is the subject of this 1973 film starring Fred Williamson.

1877. Richard Pryor costarred in this 1973 blaxploitation film.

1878. In *Coffy*, this female action hero hides razor blades in her Afro and fights drug dealers.

1879. Patti Labelle, Nona Hendryx and this woman formed LaBelle in 1973.

1870. Darrell Grant

1871. Will Marion Cook

1872. Bobby Brown

1873. Soul to Soul.

1874. Trouble Man.

1875. Jim Kelly

1876. Black Caesar

1877. The Mack

1878. Pam Grier

1879. Sara Dash

1880. His 1974 album is called *That Nigger's Crazy.*

1881. Who wrote the script for the 1975 hit, *Cooley High?*

1882. *Love to Love You Baby* was her big hit in 1975.

1883. Which ABC television special in 1977 earned the highest ratings of any network program in history?

1884. Which Yale graduate founded the Black Filmmaker Foundation in 1978?

1885. Who is the black producer of the 1978 movie, *Sgt. Pepper's Lonely Hearts Club Band*?

1886. She organized the Sugarhill label in 1979 as an important outlet for rap music.

1887. Who produced *Off the Wall* for Michael Jackson in 1979, the biggest-selling album by a black male?

1888. Who managed Kurtis Blow, the first rap artist on a major label in 1979?

1889. Which 1980 movie starring Richard Pryor and Gene Wilder earned $101 million?

1890. Wearing black panties on stage, he released *Dirty Mind,* his landmark album in 1980.

1891. Denzel Washington played in this 1981 Pulitzer Prize-winning play by Charles Fuller.

1880. Richard Pryor	*1886.* Sylvia Robinson
1881. Eric Monte	*1887.* Quincy Jones
1882. Donna Summer	*1888.* Russell Simmons
1883. Roots	*1889. Stir Crazy*
1884. Warrington Hudlin	*1890.* Prince
1885. Michael Schultz	*1891. A Soldier's Story*

1892. Who sang "And I Am Telling You I'm Not Going" in the 1981 play, *Dreamgirls?*

1893. Which album released by Michael Jackson in 1982 sold 40 million worldwide?

1894. Which play by August Wilson and starring ex-con Charles Dutton opened in 1984?

1895. Considered the best ballad singer of his generation, Luther Vandross released this album in 1985.

1896. Name Whitney Houston's first album, released in 1985.

1897. This 1986 album by Anita Baker established her as formidable pop-jazz vocalist.

1898. What is the title of Keenan Wayans' 1988 blaxploitation spoof featuring Jim Brown and Isaac Hayes?

1899. Name the 1988 movie starring Danny Glover and Mel Gibson which earned $65 million.

1900. Which Los Angeles rhythm and blues station was the first in the country to change to an all-rap format in 1984?

1901. Who produced and directed the television series, *A Different World?*

1892. Jennifer Holliday

1893. *Thriller*

1894. *Ma Rainey's Black Bottom*

1895. *The Night I Fell In Love*

1896. *Whitney*

1897. *Rapture*

1898. *I'm Gonna Git You, Sucka*

1899. *Lethal Weapon*

1900. KDAY

1901. Debbie Allen

1902. Will Smith starred in this NBC sitcom produced by Quincy Jones in 1990.

1903. Directed by Melvin Van Peebles and his son, Mario, this 1991 film featured Wesley Snipes and Ice-T.

1904. In this tribute to 1960s r&b groups, Robert Townsend acted in and directed the movie.

1905. Who is the female star in Bill Duke's 1991 film, *A Rage in Harlem*?

1906. This 1991 film by 23-year-old John Singleton features Larry Fishburne as the caring father.

1907. In 1956 she made the first of several "Songbook" recordings for Verve, the new label started by . impresario Norman Granz.

1908. In 1936 at the Congress Hotel in Chicago, with whom did Lionel Hampton and Teddy Wilson sit in with to integrate jazz for the first time?

1909. What song was Charlie Parker playing in 1939 at a Harlem jam session when he discovered the harmonic changes that lead to be-bop?

1910. She convinced her husband, Louis Armstrong, to leave King Oliver's band and go out on his own.

1911. A pianist who wrote for Andy Kirk and the Mighty Clouds of Joy, she became one of America's most respected composers.

1912. This vibist's band called Ubiquity offered an acid-jazz style in the 1970s.

1913. In a four-year period from 1974 to 1977, they scored r&b hits like "Fire" and "Love Rollercoaster."

1914. Which jazz pianist, accompanied by Charley Haden on bass and Roy Haynes on drums, released *Wanton Spirit* in 1995?

1915. This 18-year-old trumpet player joined Art Blakey & the Jazz Messengers in 1980.

1916. From New Orleans, he replaced Wynton Marsalis as the trumpet player for Art Blakey & the Jazz Messengers in 1982.

1917. In a 70-year career, this alto saxophonist played everything from swing to bebop, and wrote standards like "When Lights Are Low."

1918. Who is the 26-year-old saxophonist from Detroit who focused on jazz standards in his 1995 album, *Jurassic Classics' Real Quiet Storm*?

1911. Mary Lou Williams

1912. Roy Ayers

1913. The Ohio Players

1914. Kenny Barron

1915. Wynton Marsalis

1916. Terence Blanchard

1917. Benny Carter

1918. James Carter

1919. Name the circuit of 80 theaters between Philadelphia and Texas responsible for most black musical entertainment in the 1920s and 1930s.

1920. This tenor sax player's nickname was Bean.

1921. While in Oklahoma in 1925, he formed the Blue Devils, the innovative territorial band that emphasized a modern rhythm section.

1922. What did the Blue Devils, an important Oklahoma band in the 1920s, call their music?

1923. What is the title of sassy jazz vocalist Nancy Wilson's 1969 influential album?

1924. Hard bop saxophonist Hank Mobley produced this melodic album in 1960.

1925. Gene Ammons, accompanied by Ray Barretto on congas, produced this powerful album in 1960.

1926. Name the 1963 debut album which includes "Blue Bossa" by saxist Joe Henderson.

1927. This early 1960 album by guitarist Wes Montgomery introduced several of his celebrated compositions.

1928. In 1943 during his first annual Carnegie Hall program, Duke Ellington premiered this composition.

1919. Theater Owners Booking Association

1920. Coleman Hawkins

1921. Walter Page

1922. gutbucket

1923. But Beautiful

1924. Soul Station

1925. Boss Tenor

1926. Page One

1927. The Incredible Guitar of Wes Montgomery

1928. "Black, Brown and Beige"

1929. Which record by Cassandra Wilson was on the *Billboard* list of 10 top sellers in 1994?

1930. Christened the High Priest of be-bop, he appeared on the cover of *Time* magazine in 1964.

1931. This 1969 Miles Davis album of jazz-rock fusion sold 500,000 copies.

1932. In what year did Sidney Bechet relocate to Paris?

1933. Which jazz saxophonist, a Harvard College *summa cum laude* graduate, released two albums in 1993?

1934. In 1979, when this 56-year-old jazz great died in Cuernavaca, 56 whales beached themselves on the Mexican coast.

1935. This record by Lena Horne was one of *Billboard's* 10 top-sellers in 1994.

1936. The album by Cyrus Chestnut was considered one of the 10 best in 1994 by the *New York Times*.

1937. The real name of this famed blues singer born in Baltimore was Eleanor Fagan.

1938. Which was the first black spiritual choral group to sing in scheduled radio broadcasts in the 1940s?

1929. Blue Light Til Dawn

1930. Thelonius Monk

1931. Bitches Brew

1932. 1951

1933. Joshua Redman

1934. Charles Mingus

1935. We'll Be Together Again

1936. Revelation

1937. Billie Holiday

1938. The Wings Over Jordan

1939. She was the first African-American woman to make gospel records during the 1930s and 1940s.

1940. This African-American comedian, best known for his comic poems, was featured in the movie, *The Wiz*.

1941. In what year did amateur night at New York's famed Apollo Theater begin?

1942. This trumpeter with Duke Ellington helped popularize the Zoot suit.

1943. Dubbed the "Black Garbo," she was the first black actress to receive a multi-year contract with MGM.

1944. Former dean of the School of Communications at Howard University, he directed *The White Girl* in 1990, about drug abuse and self hatred.

1945. Considered the greatest blues composer ever, he wrote more than 500 songs including "I'm Your Hoochie Coochie Man," and "Little Red Rooster."

1946. The hymn, "Lift Ev'ry Voice and Sing," by James Weldon Johnson, was meant to celebrate whose birthday?

1947. This Atlanta-based funk group produced the hit "Tennessee" in the early 1990s.

1948. Which songstress fronted the George Duke Orchestra at the Kennedy Center in Washington, DC to benefit the Democratic National Committee in 1991?

1949. One of the few rhythm and blues singers who scats, his falsetto swoops and glides on ballads like "You Are My Lady."

1950. With Dorothy Donegan and Sweets Edison, singer Betty Carter was named a Jazz Master by which organization in 1991?

1951. The 1992 musical, *Five Guys Names Moe* is based on the life of this singer/comedian/saxophonist who had five million-selling records in the 1940s and '50s.

1952. Winner of a 1989 Tony for Broadway's *Black and Blue* revue, she was Atlantic Record's biggest hit maker from 1949 to 1962.

1953. Name the country music singer who received a standing ovation at the 1991 Celebrate the Soul of American Music awards.

1954. Who is considered the father of the modern jazz trombone whose 1988 concert at the Village Vanguard was his first New York appearance in 20 years?

1955. His 1990 album, *Live at the Blue Note* won a Grammy for this legendary pianist with the dizzying technique.

1948. Anita Baker

1949. Freddie Jackson

1950. The National Endowment for the Arts

1951. Louis Jordan

1952. Ruth Brown

1953. Charley Pride

1954. J. J. Johnson

1955. Oscar Peterson

1956. Called the godfather of jazz, this drummer who died in 1990 trained nearly every top jazz star performing today.

1957. Who is the producer of New Orleans Jazzfest, which began in 1970 with 200 ticketholders and now hosts at least 300,000?

1958. Considered the best sax player in jazz, he released *Falling in Love with Jazz* in 1990.

1959. She made the first vocal album of Thelonious Monk tunes in 1990 with *Carmen Sings Monk.*

1960. Called Dr. Jazz, this pianist is the first jazz musician appointed to the National Council on the Arts.

1961. This classic vocal quintet is responsible for hits like "One of a Kind," "It's A Shame," "I'll Be Around" and the Dionne Warwick collaboration, "Then Came You."

1962. The pyrotechnical brilliance of this pianist who has influenced artists from Oscar Peterson to Stevie Wonder was evident in a 7-CD set in 1991, *The Complete Pablo Solo Masterpieces.*

1963. This renowed quartet was best known for its elegant expressions like *Django* and *Softly as in a Morning Sunrise.*

1956. Art Blakey	*1960.* Billy Taylor
1957. Quint Davis	*1961.* The Spinners
1958. Sonny Rollins	*1962.* Art Tatum
1959. Carmen McRae	*1963.* The Modern Jazz Quartet

1964. His tragicomedy, *Seven Guitars*, opened at New York's Walter Keer Theater in 1996.

1965. George C. Wolfe and Savion Glover describe black American history through tap dancing in this 1996 Broadway play.

1966. J.E. Franklin wrote this 1971 play about a bickering Texas family.

1967. This trusted lieutenant of Duke Ellington actually wrote and copyrighted "Satin Doll," "Lush Life" and "Take the A Train."

1968. Harry Belafonte co-stars in this 1995 film in which the roles of blacks and whites are reversed.

1969. He was the second black male to win an Oscar in an acting category.

1970. At 29 this pianist produced a debut album in 1995 that earned raves from the critics.

1971. After his wife and child were killed in an automobile accident in 1932, he composed "Take My Hand, Precious Lord," the most popular sacred composition ever written by a black American.

1972. A legendary singer of the blues until she died at age 89, she wrote "Down Hearted Blues" in 1922.

1964. August Wilson

1965. *Bring in Da Noise, Bring in Da Funk*

1966. *Black Girl*

1967. Billy Strayhorn

1968. *White Man's Burden*

1969. Denzel Washington

1970. Jacky Terrason

1971. Thomas Dorsey

1972. Alberta Hunter

1973. The Colored Players of Philadelphia produced this film that many consider the finest race movie of its time in 1927.

1974. He was a pioneer producer of race movies from 1918–48.

1975. Paul Robeson's first movie role in 1924 was in this film.

1976. They produced the 1968 Janet Jackson album, *Control*.

1977. He played Bigger Thomas in this French-produced film of *Native Son* in 1951.

1978. This was one of four dramatic weekly network series featuring blacks that premiered in 1988 and starred Howard Rollins.

1979. This publicist represented Eddie Murphy, Essence Communications and others.

1980. He was publicist for Michael Jackson's production company, MJJ, Inc.

1981. Who released a series of "sermon" songs like "Keep on Pushing" in the 1960s?

1982. By the time his "A Change Is Gonna Come" was released as a single, he had been shot to death.

1973. The Scar of Shame

1974. Oscar Micheaux

1975. Body and Soul

1976. Terry Lewis and Jimmy Jam Harris

1977. Richard Wright

1978. In the Heat of the Night

1979. Terrie M. Williams

1980. Bob Jones

1981. Curtis Mayfield

1982. Sam Cooke

1983. Which movie with comic Eddie Murphy in 1983 earned $90 million?

1984. They recorded "Earth Angel" in the 1950s before it was popularized by the Crew Cuts.

1985. She recorded "Hound Dog" before Elvis Presley.

1986. Although the McGuire Sisters made it commercially successful, "Sincerely" was first recorded by this 1950s doo wop group.

1987. Who recorded "I Almost Lost My Mind in the 1950s before Pat Boone made it a commercial success?

1988. *The Cosby Show* about an upper middle-class black family debuts in what year?

1989. He was drum major for James Reese Europe's sensational World War II military band.

1990. Her free concert in NewYork's Central Park in 1983 was marred by youth muggings and crime.

1991. How many Grammy awards did Michael Jackson win for his 1984 album, *Thriller?*

1992. They were the backup group for the historic 1920 Mamie Smith recording of "Crazy Blues."

1983. Trading Places	*1988.* 1984
1984. The Penguins	*1989.* Bill "Bojangles" Robinson
1985. Big Mama Thornton	*1990.* Diana Ross
1986. The Moonglows	*1991.* Eight
1987. Ivory Joe Hunter	*1992.* The Jazz Hounds

1993. Who was W.C. Handy's partner in the founding of Black Swan records in 1921?

1994. This Texan was the best-selling bluesman of the 1920s, recording 75 songs for Paramount.

1995. Based at Harlem's Savoy Ballroom, he showcased a young vocalist named Ella Fitzgerald in the 1930s.

1996. Who was the genius arranger for Jimmy Lunceford's band based at the Cotton Club in the mid-thirties?

1997. He helped make the guitar the dominant instrument for rock and roll artists.

1998. This hit by Chubby Checker is the only record to reach the top spot on the pop charts twice — in 1960 and in 1962.

1999. Beginning in 1964, they produced a string of 15 hit singles in a row including "Soldier Boy" and "Mama Said"

1993. Harvey Pace   *1997.* Chuck Berry

1994. Blind Lemon Jefferson   *1998.* "The Twist"

1995. Chick Webb   *1999.* The Shirelles

1996. Sy Oliver

Bibliography

Readers may find the following works helpful for obtaining additional information about African-American historical achievement.

Ashe, Arthur. *A Hard Road to Glory: The History of the African-American Athlete.* 3 vols. New York: Warner Books, 1988.

Aptheker, H.A. *Documentary History of the Negro People in the United States.* NewYork: Citadel Press, 1951.

Baker, Theodore. *Baker's Biographical Dictionary of Musicians.* 8th ed. New York: Macmillan Publishing Co., 1992.

Bennett, Lerone Jr. *Pioneers in Protest.* New York: Penguin Books, 1968.

Bird, Christiane. *The Jazz and Blues Lover's Guide to the U.S.* New York: Addison-Wesley, 1991.

Brawley, Benjamin. *Negro Builders and Heroes.* Chapel Hill: University of North Carolina Press, 1937.

Christian, Charles M. *Black Saga: The African American Experience.* New York: Houghton Mifflin, 1995.

Collins, Charles M., and David Cohen, eds. *The African Americans.* New York: Penguin Books, Inc., 1993.

Dates, Jannette, and William Barlow. *Split Image: African Americans in the Mass Media.* Washington, D.C.: Howard University Press, 1993.

Davis, John P. *The American Negro Reference Book.* Englewood Cliffs, N.J.: Prentice-Hall, 1966.

Estell, Kenneth. *African America: Portrait of a People.* New York: Visible Ink Press, 1994.

Floyd, Samuel. *Black Music in the Harlem Renaissance; A Collection of Essays.* New York: Greenwood, 1990.

Franklin, John Hope. *From Slavery to Freedom.* New York: Alfred A. Knopf, 1956.

Gutman, Bill. *The Pictorial History of Basketball.* New York: Gallery, 1988.

Haber, Louis. *Black Pioneers of Science and Invention*. New York: Harcourt Brace, 1970.

Hampton, Henry, and Steve Fayer. *Voices of Freedom: An Oral History of the Civil Rights Movement from the 1950s through the 1980s*. New York: Bantam Books, Inc., 1990.

Harley, Sharon. *The Timetables of African-American History*. New York: Simon & Schuster, 1995.

Harris, Sheldon. *Blues Who's Who*. New York: Da Capo Press, 1979.

Hine, Darlene Clark, ed. *Black Women in America: An Historical Encyclopedia*. 2 Vols. Brooklyn: Carlson Publishing, 1993.

Joyce, Donald. *Blacks in the Humanities, 1750–1984; A Selected Annotated Bibliography*. New York: Greenwood Press, 1986.

The Kaiser Index to Black Resources, 1948–1986. 5 Vols. Brooklyn: Carlson Pub.,1992.

Leab, Daniel J. *From Sambo to Superspade: The Black Experience in Motion Pictures*. Boston: Houghton Mifflin, 1975.

Newman, Richard. *Black Index: Afro-Americans in Selected Periodicals, 1907–1949*. New York: Garland, 1981.

Osofsky, Gilbert. *Harlem: The Making of a Ghetto*. New York: Harper and Row, 1963.

Riis, Thomas. *Just before Jazz: Black Musical Theatre in New York, 1890–1915*. Washington, D.C.: Smithsonian Press, 1989.

Rust, Edna, and Art Rust. *Art Rust's Illustrated History of the Black Athlete*. New York: Doubleday, 1985.

Santelli, Robert. *Big Book of the Blues*. New York: Penguin Books, 1993.

Time-Life editors. *Voices of Triumph*. 3 vols. Alexandria, Va.: Time-Life Books, Inc., 1993.

Woll, Allen. *Black Musical Theatre: From Coontown to Dreamgirls*. Baton Rouge: Louisiana State University Press, 1989.

Index